I make portraits of bicycles in my studio in Brooklyn, NYC. I first began painting bicycles in 1996, though I've always ridden one.

I discovered painting in a high school illustration class, and decided in one week that I was going to be an artist. So I studied painting at the Boston Museum School and earned my MFA at the New York Academy of Art. Then I worked for many years as a decorative painter while always working on my own art work too. I painted my first bicycle picture in 1996. I had started riding a bike around New York City and noticed how beautiful it was, both the bike and the riding. It inspired me to paint bikes. I kept painting portraits of bicycles because I'm still fascinated by the stories behind them and their beauty.

I have never owned a car, and get wherever I need to go by bike. On a bicycle I can see the city, breathe fresh air and know I'm not polluting by getting where I need to go. Getting around using my own energy makes me happy and keeps me healthy. Most of my friends ride bikes, too.

The bicycles I paint belong to friends, patrons, and sometimes to famous cyclists. Each bicycle is part of someone's life, and I loves to think about how each bicycle has been ridden and loved by the person who owns it. Everyone's bicycle carries a story, and a little bit of that story is painted into a portrait of that bicycle.

You can learn more about my work at BicyclePaintings.com or write to me at taliah@bicyclepaintings.com.

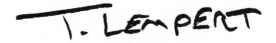

THE CLASSIC BICYCLE COLORING BOOK

For a catalog, write
Microcosm Publishing
2752 N. Williams Ave
Portland, OR 97227
or visit MicrocosmPublishing.com

ISBN 978-1-62106-418-3
This is Microcosm #233

Distributed worldwide by PGW and in the UK by Turnaround

Global labor conditions are bad, and our roots in industrial Cleveland in the 70s and 80s made us appreciate the need to treat workers right. Therefore, our books are **MADE IN THE USA.**

If you bought this on Amazon, I'm so sorry. You could have gotten it cheaper and supported a small, independent publisher at MicrocosmPublishing.com

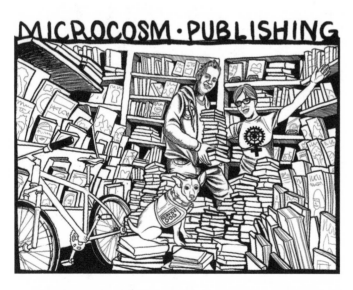

Microcosm Publishing is Portland's most diversified publishing house and distributor with a focus on the colorful, authentic, and empowering. Our books and zines have put your power in your hands since 1996, equipping readers to make positive changes in their lives and in the world around them. Microcosm emphasizes skill-building, showing hidden histories, and fostering creativity through challenging conventional publishing wisdom with books and bookettes about DIY skills, food, bicycling, gender, self-care, and social justice. What was once a distro and record label was started by Joe Biel in his bedroom and has become among the oldest independent publishing houses in Portland, OR. We are a politically moderate, centrist publisher in a world that has inched to the right for the past 80 years.

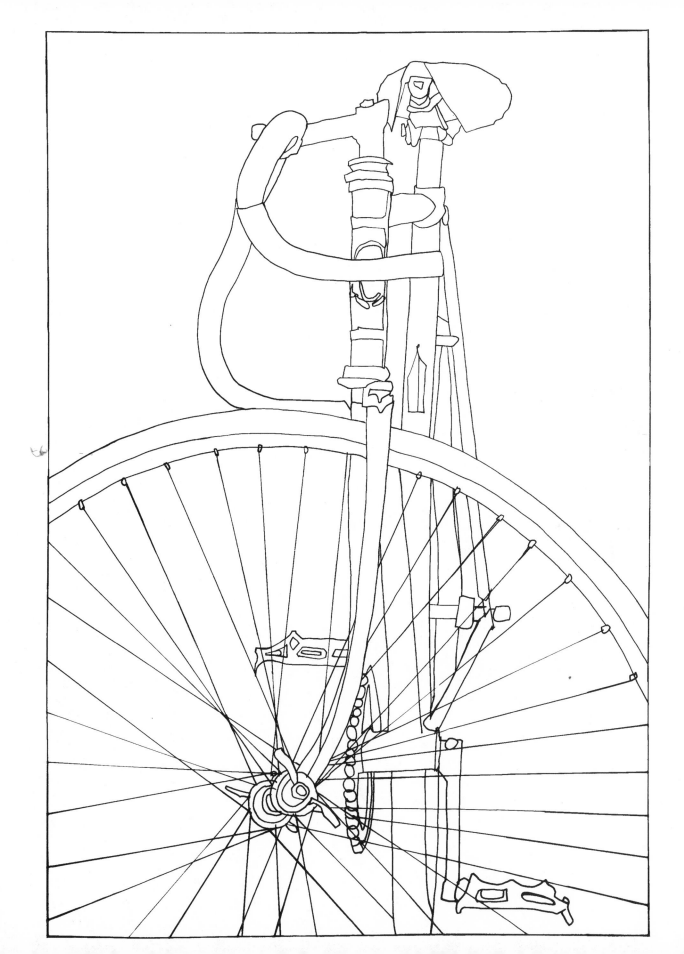

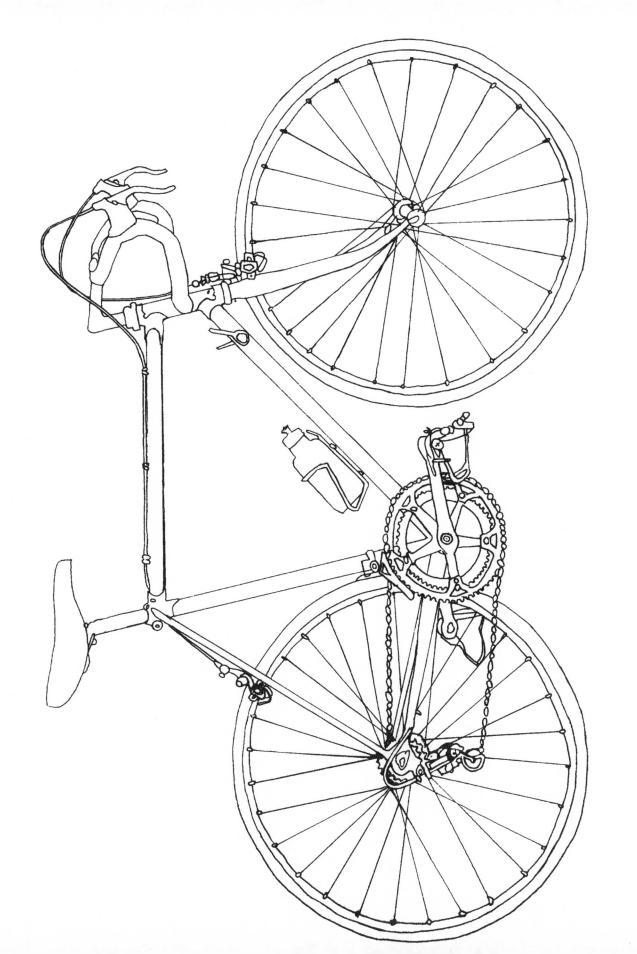

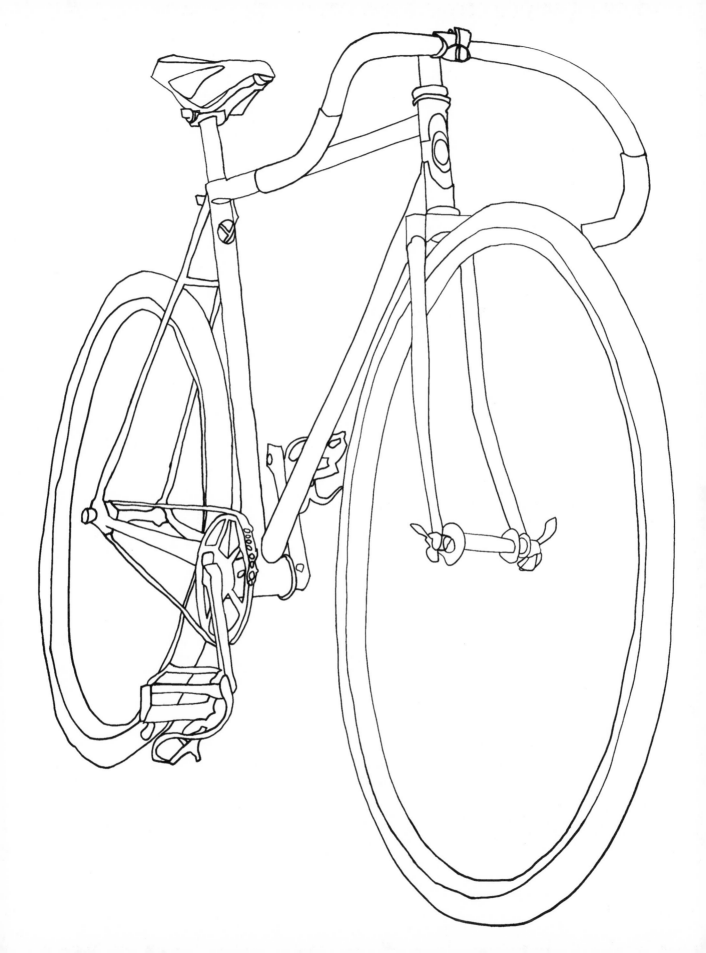

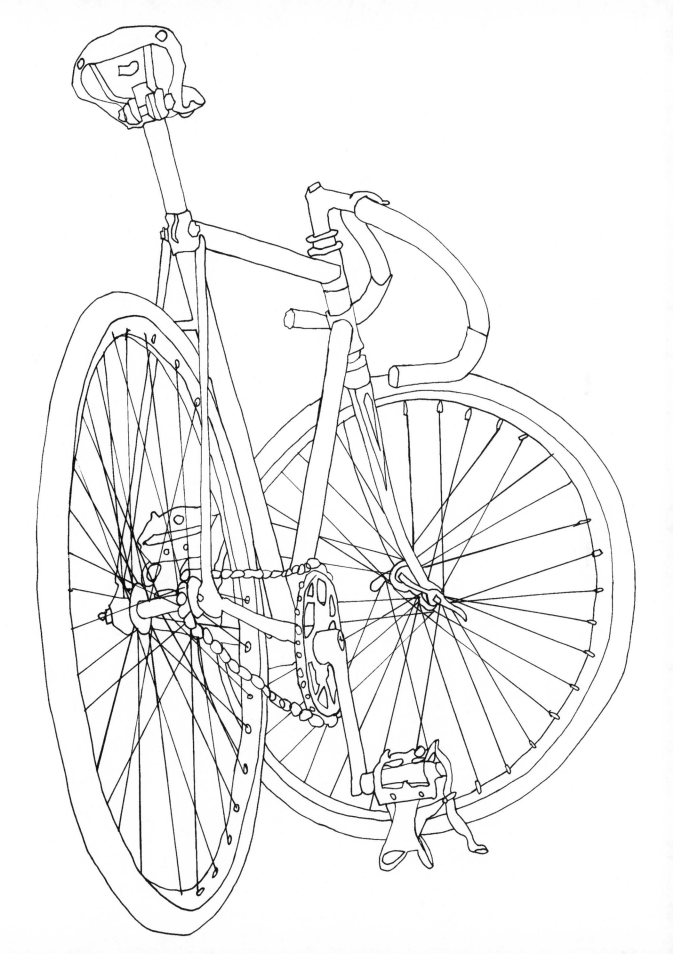

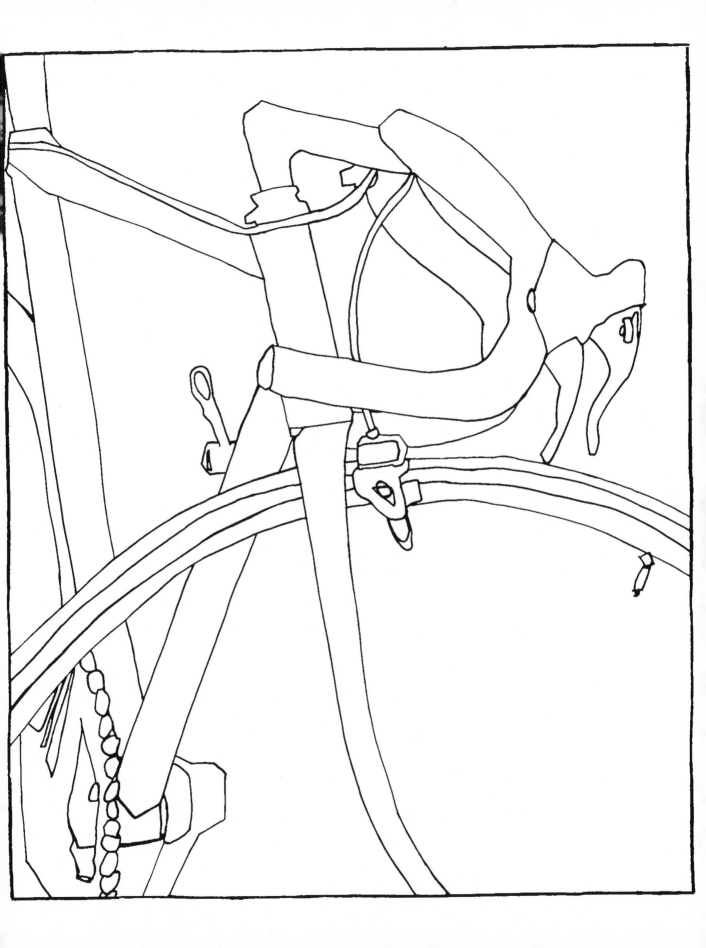

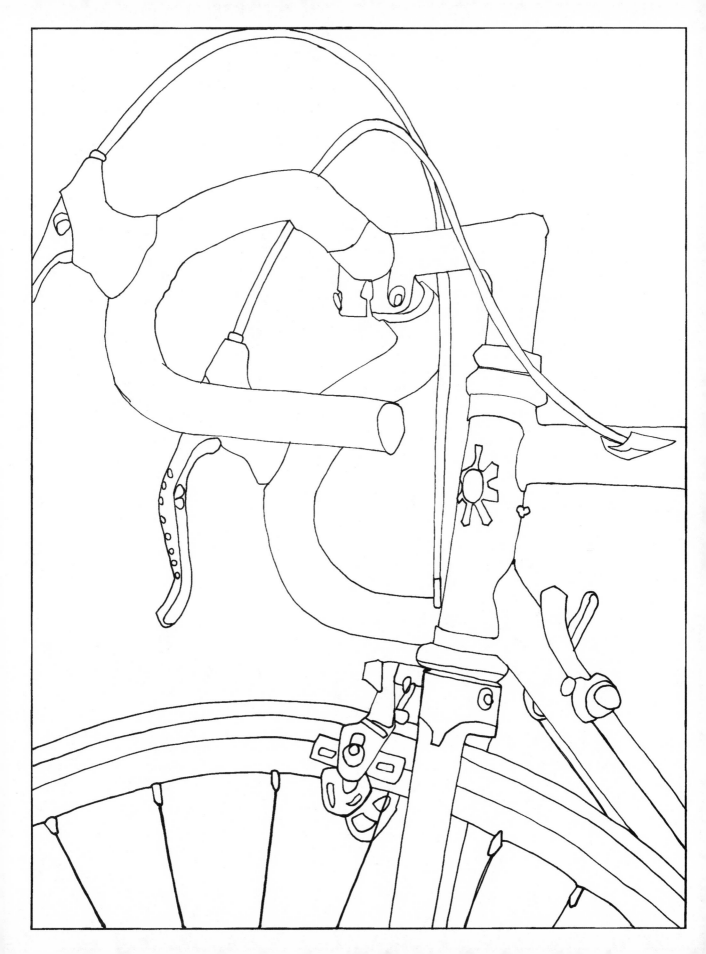

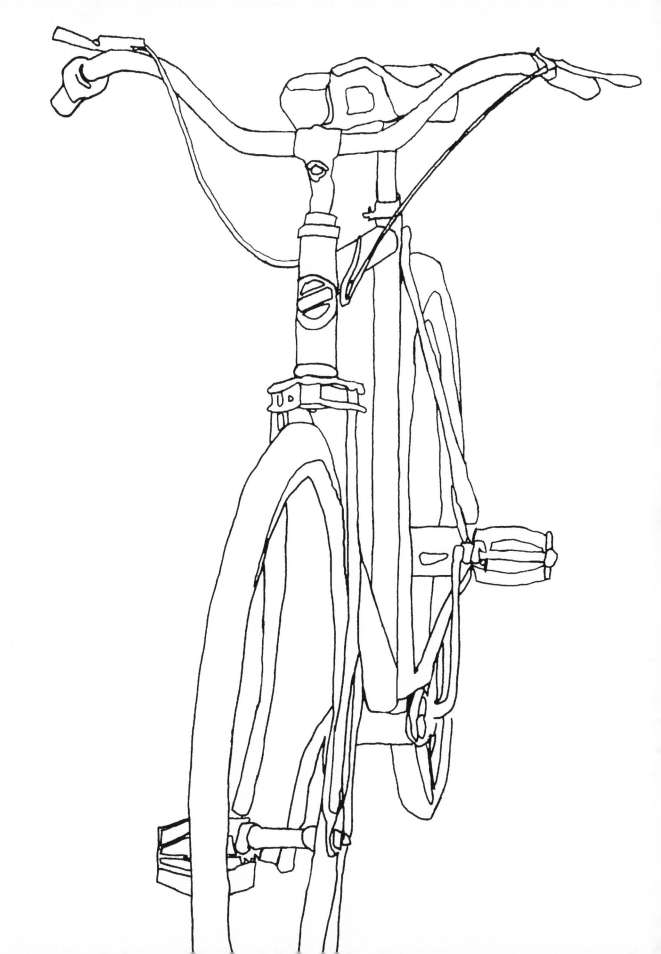

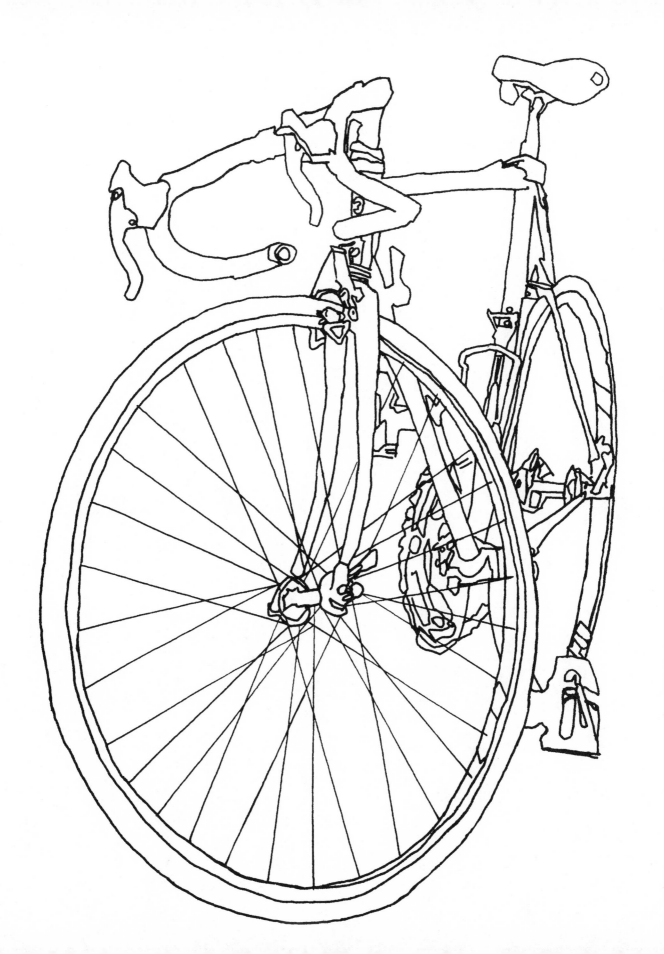

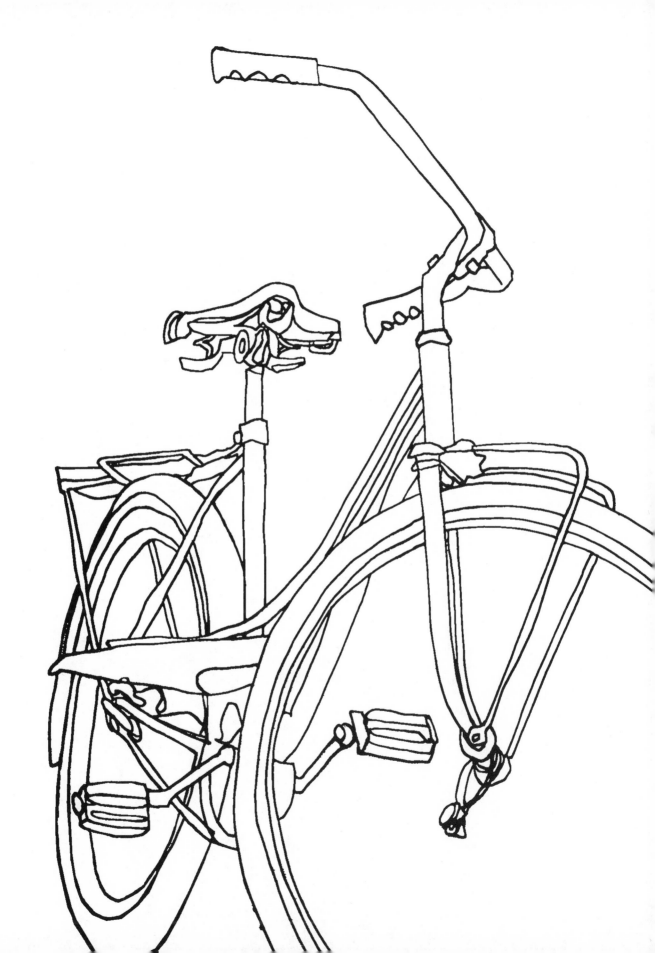

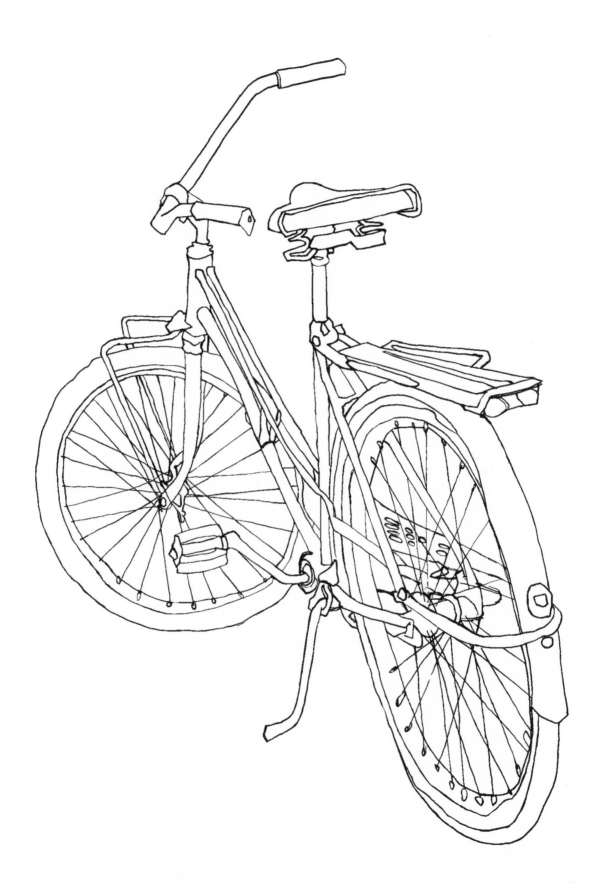

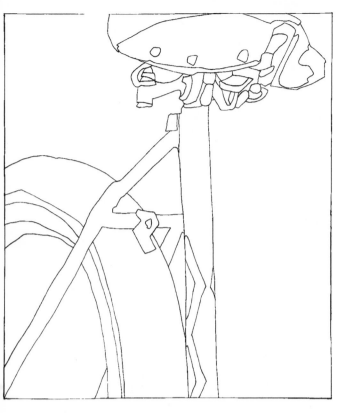
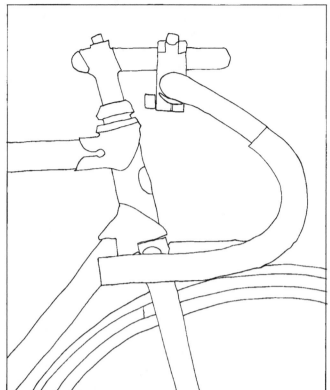
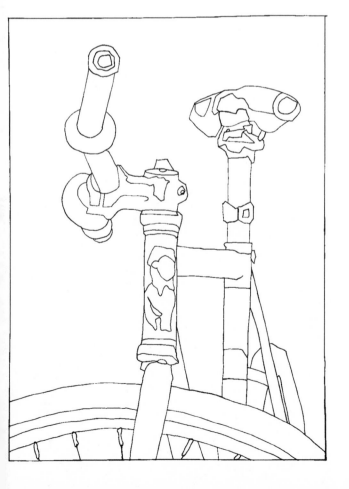
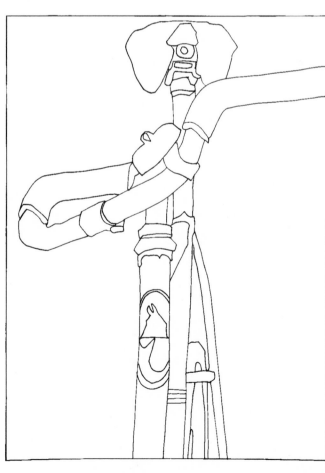

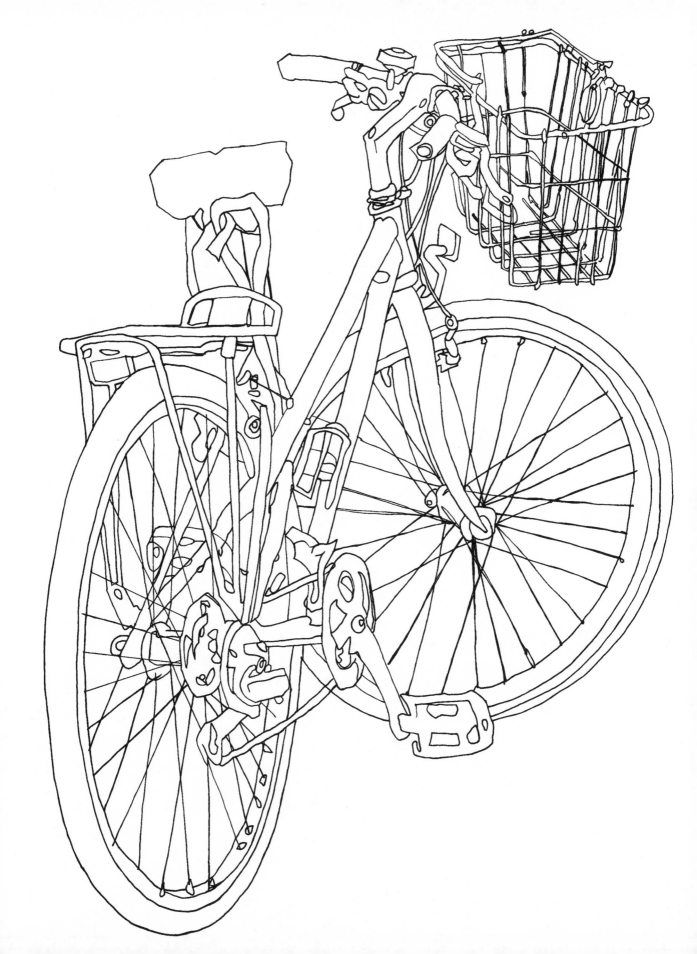

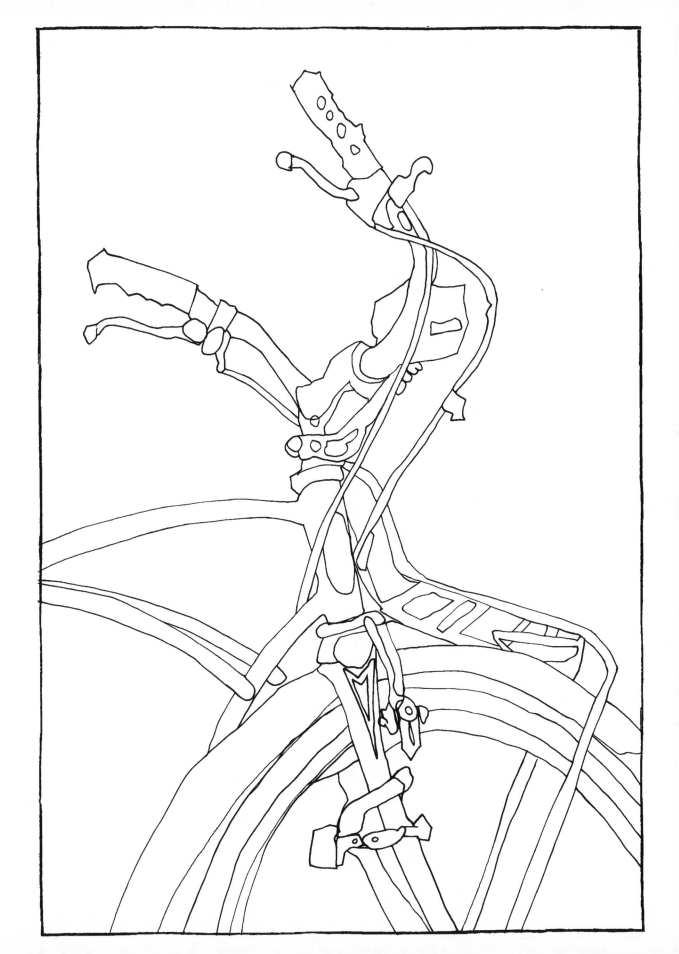

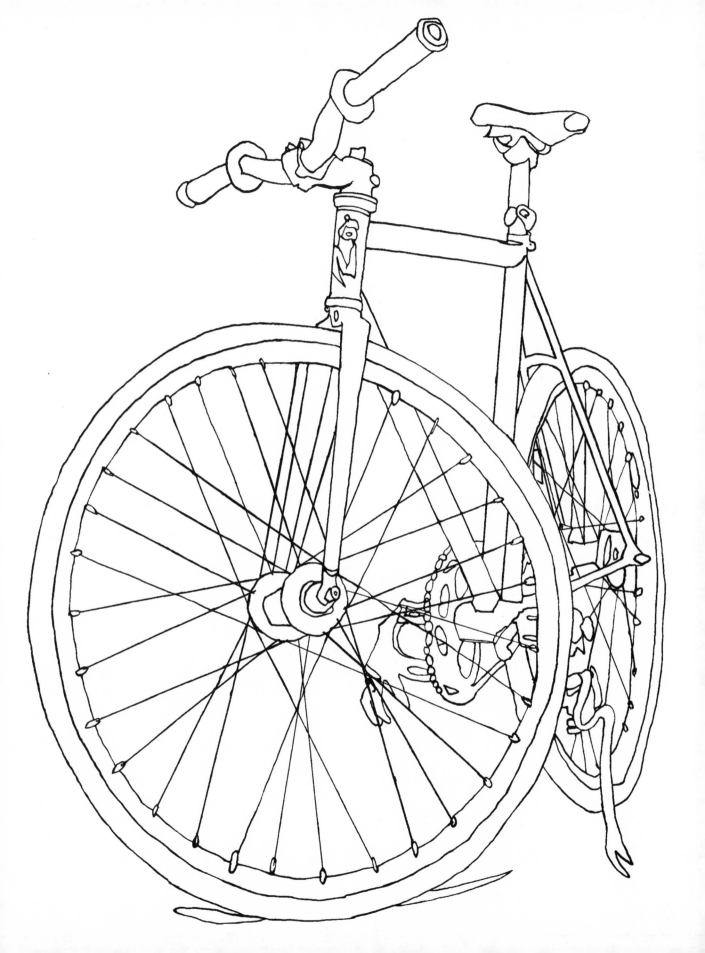

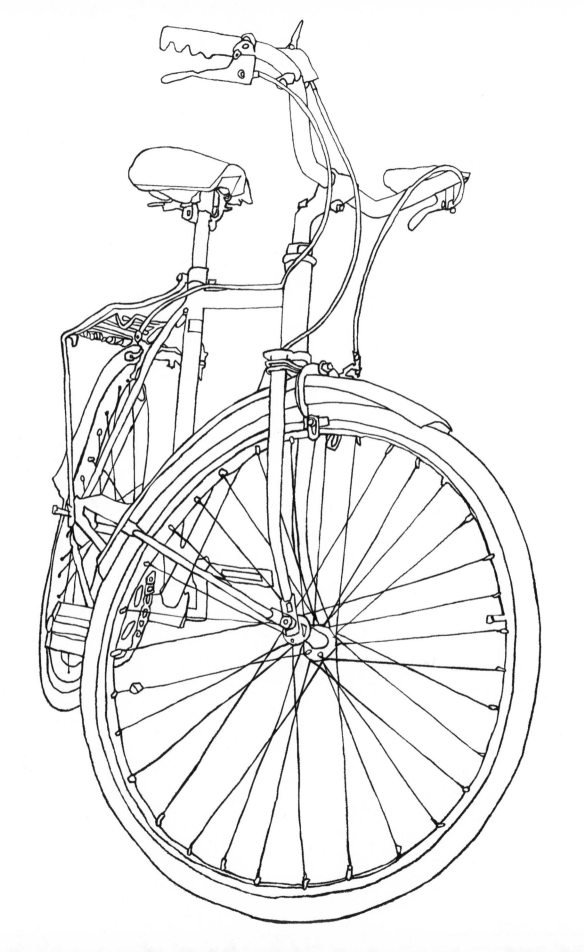

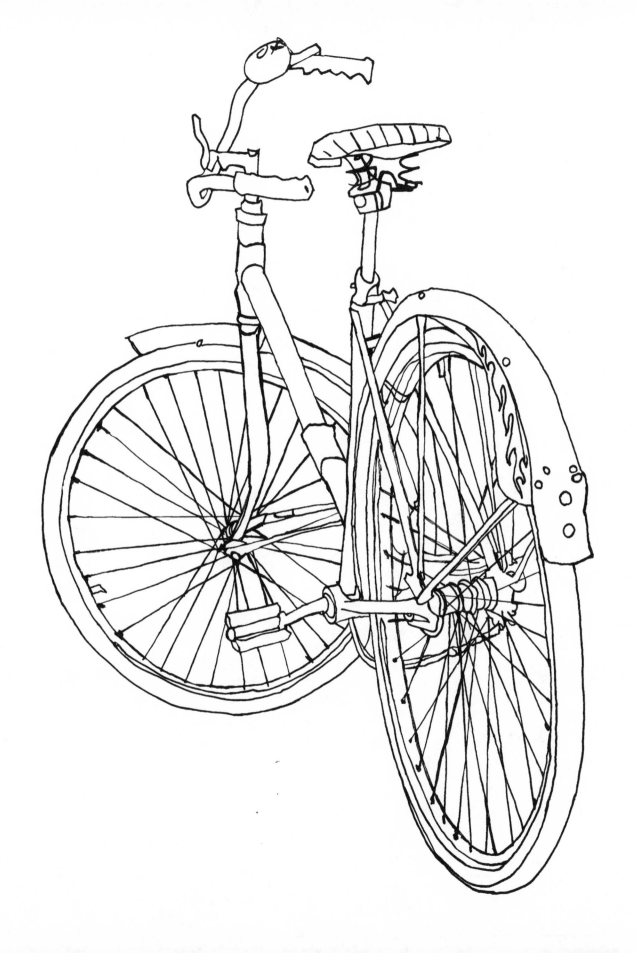

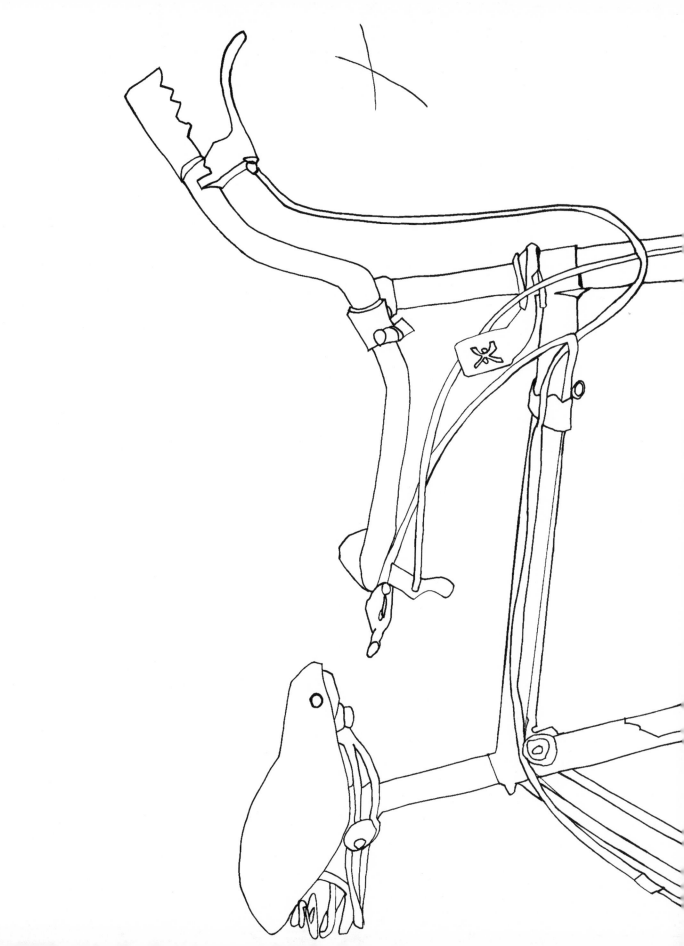

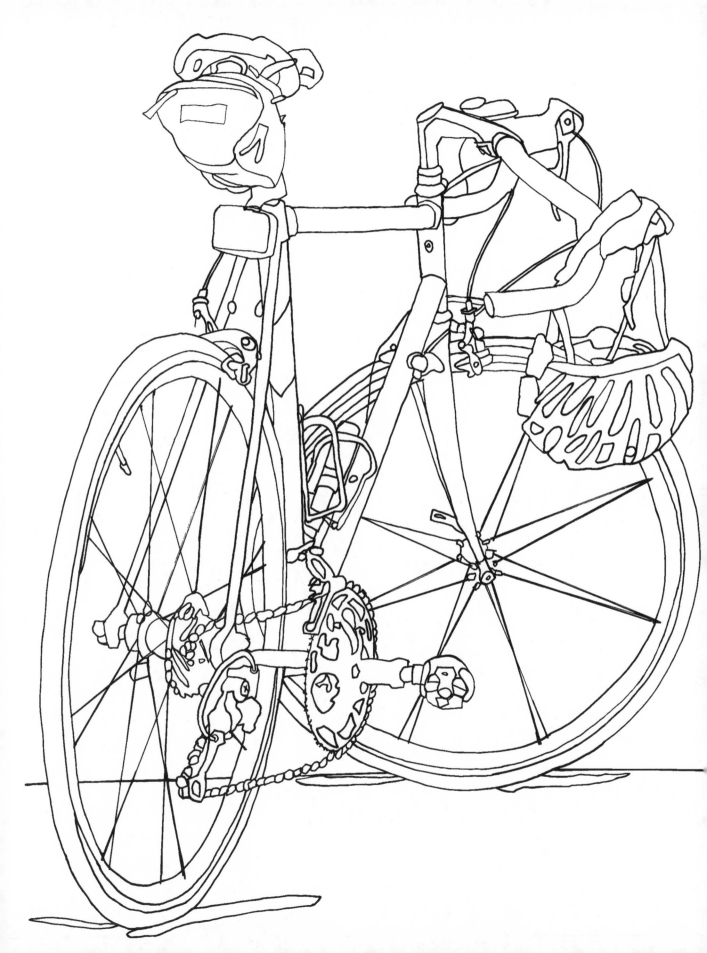

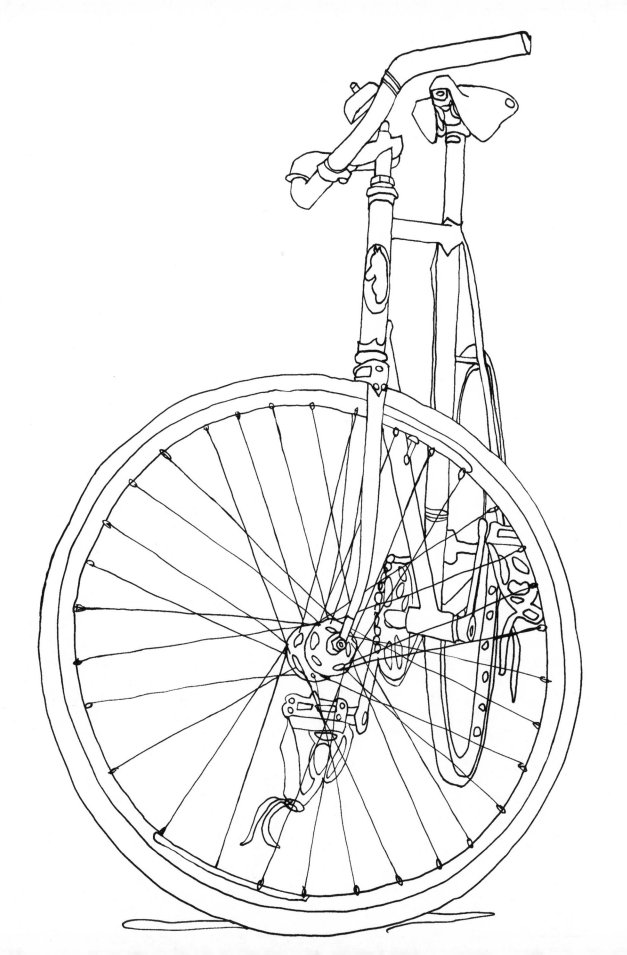

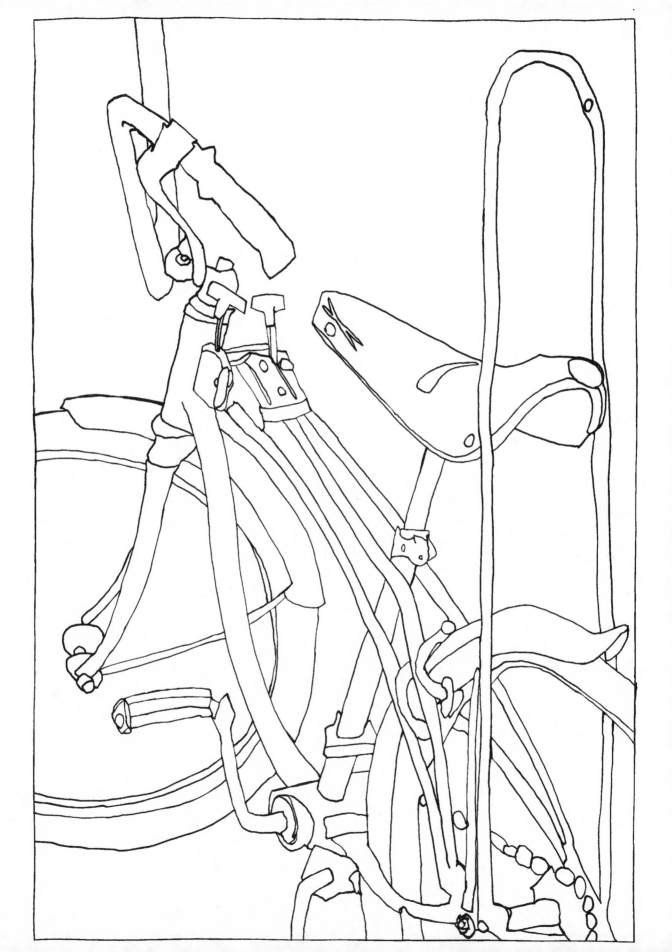

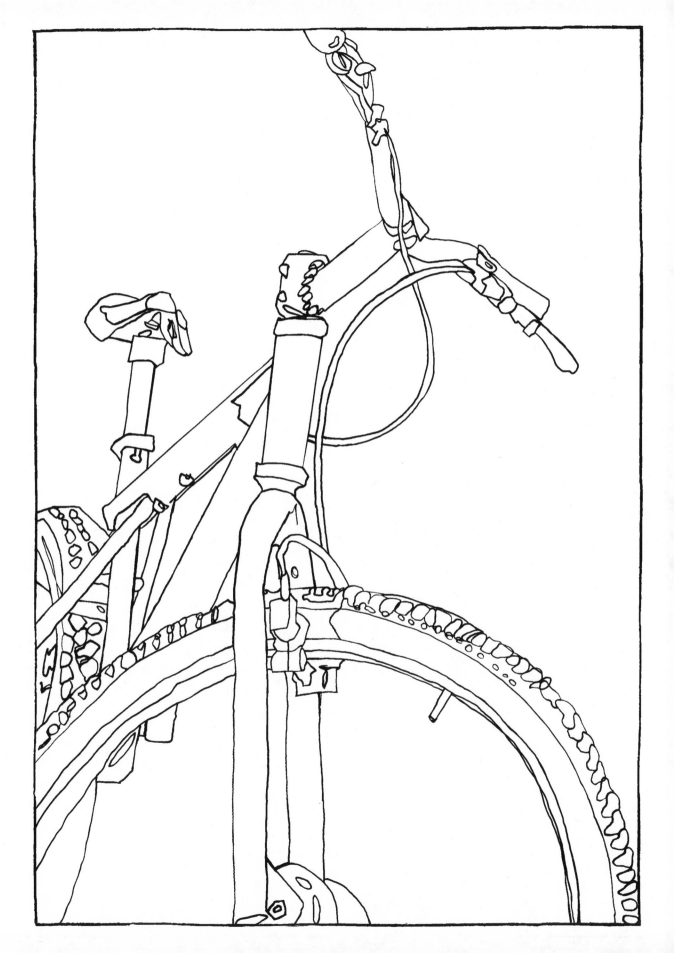

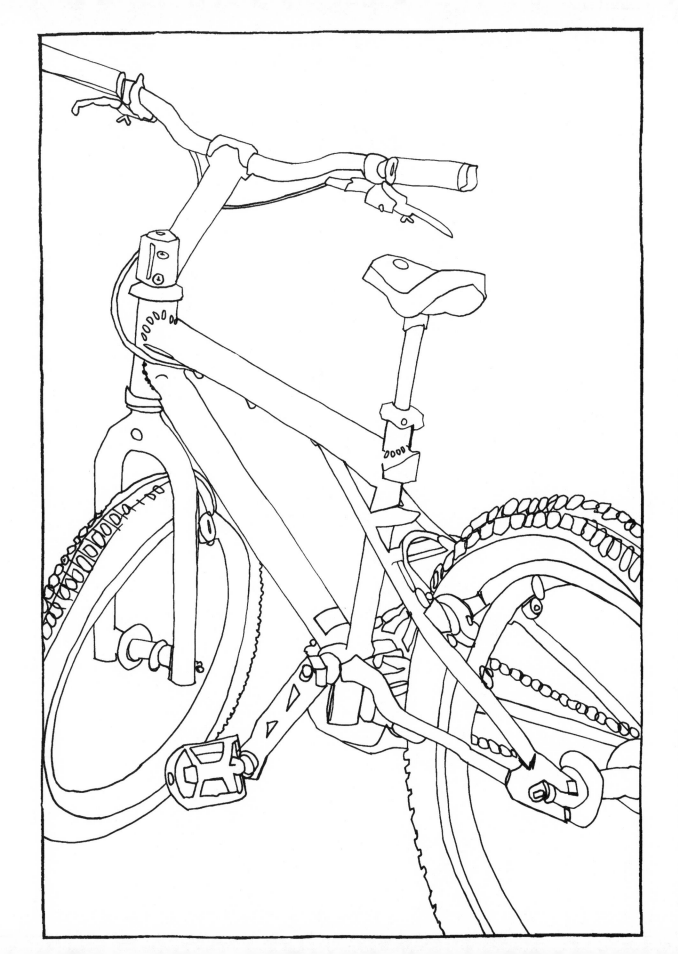

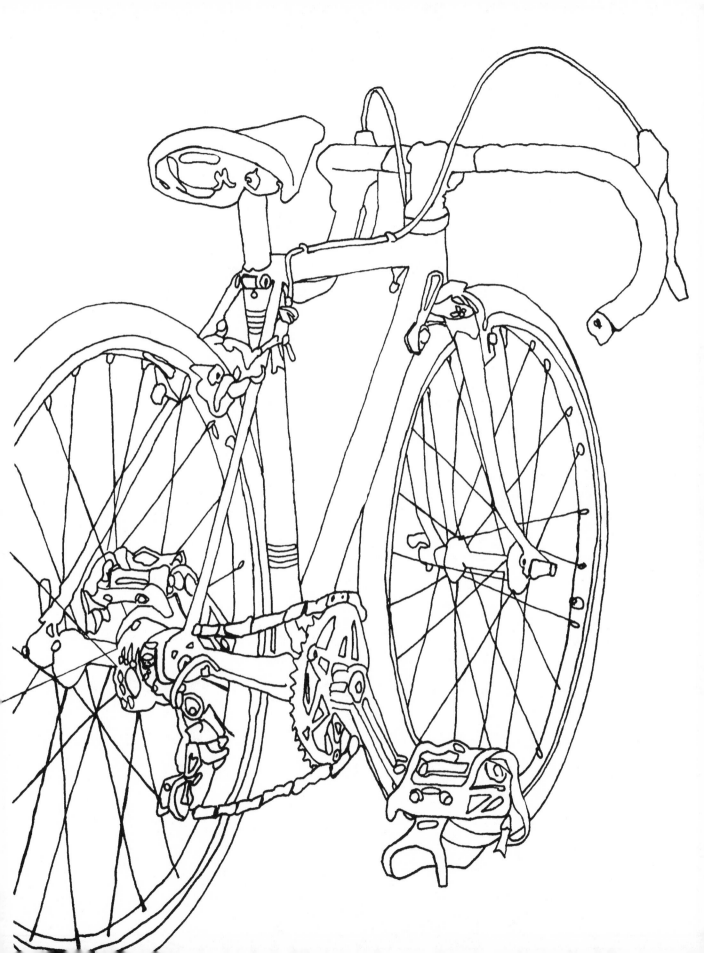

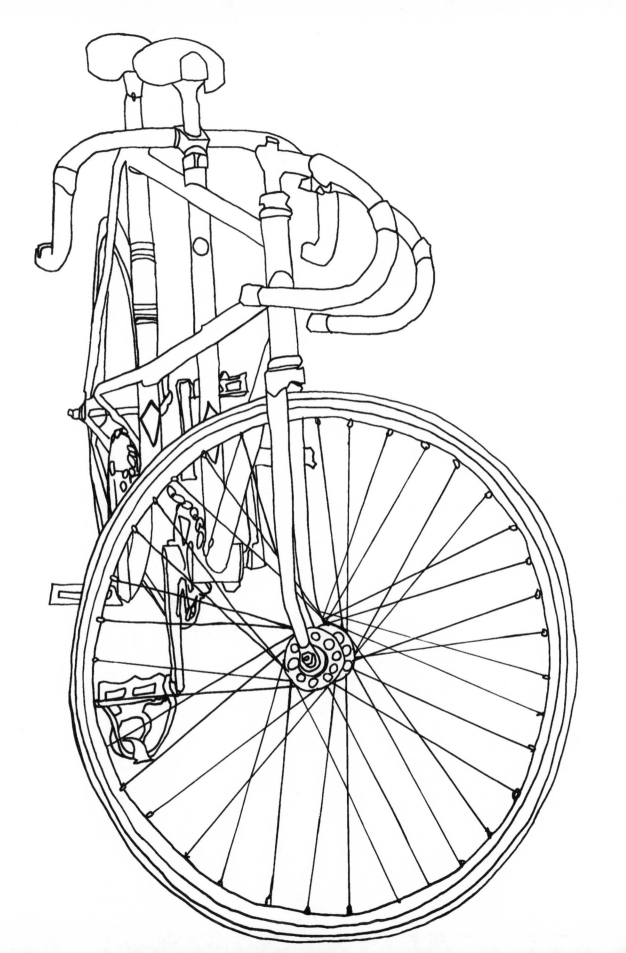

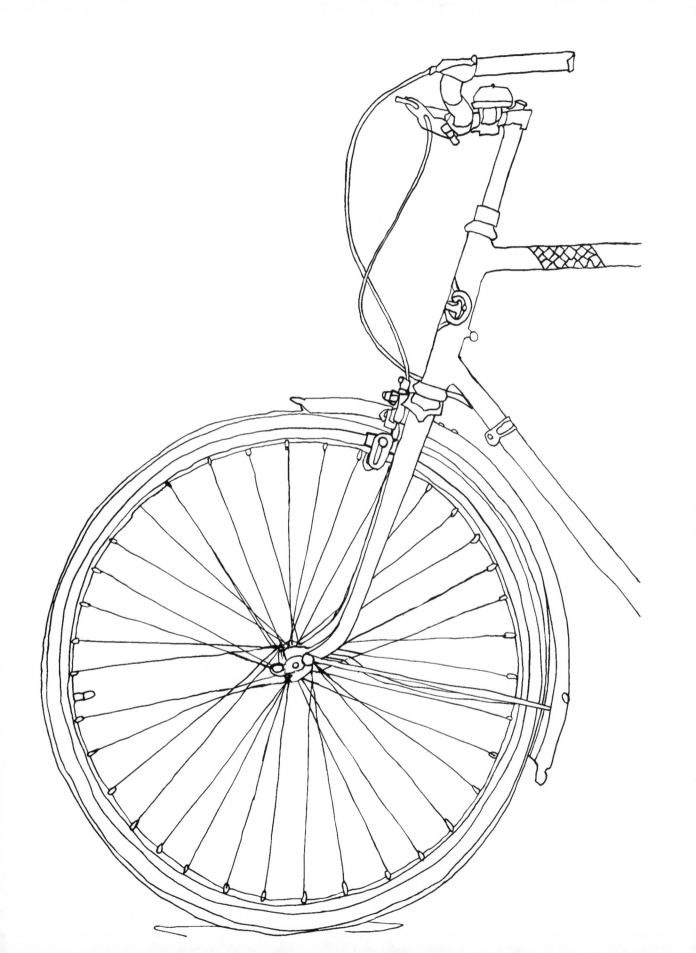

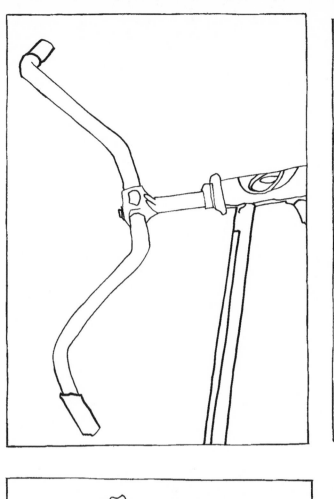

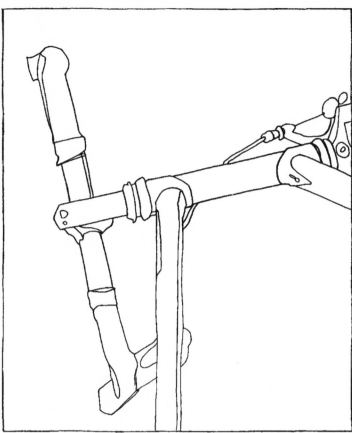

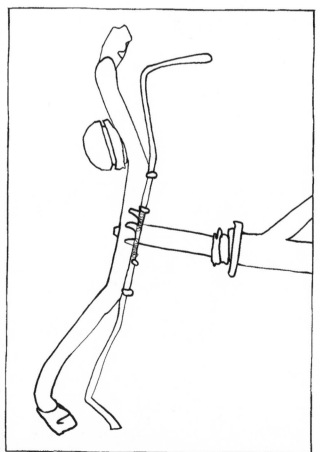

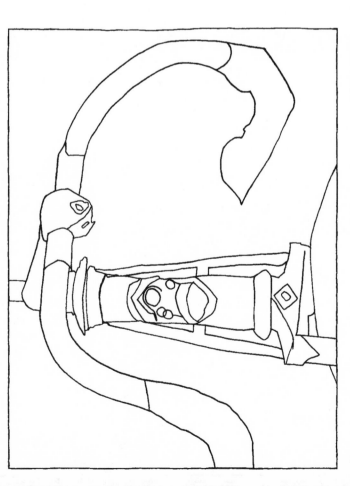

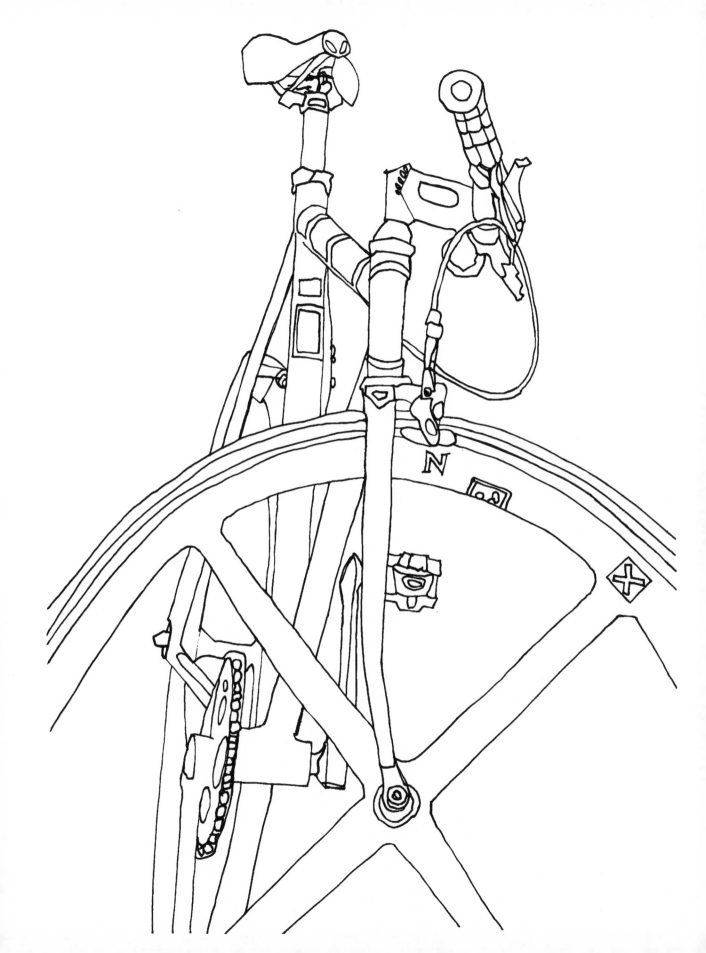

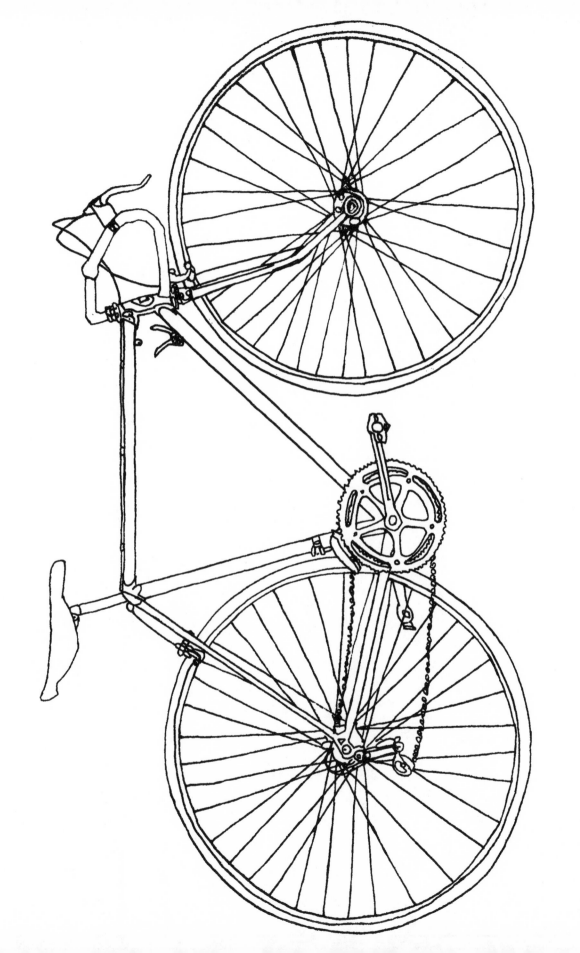

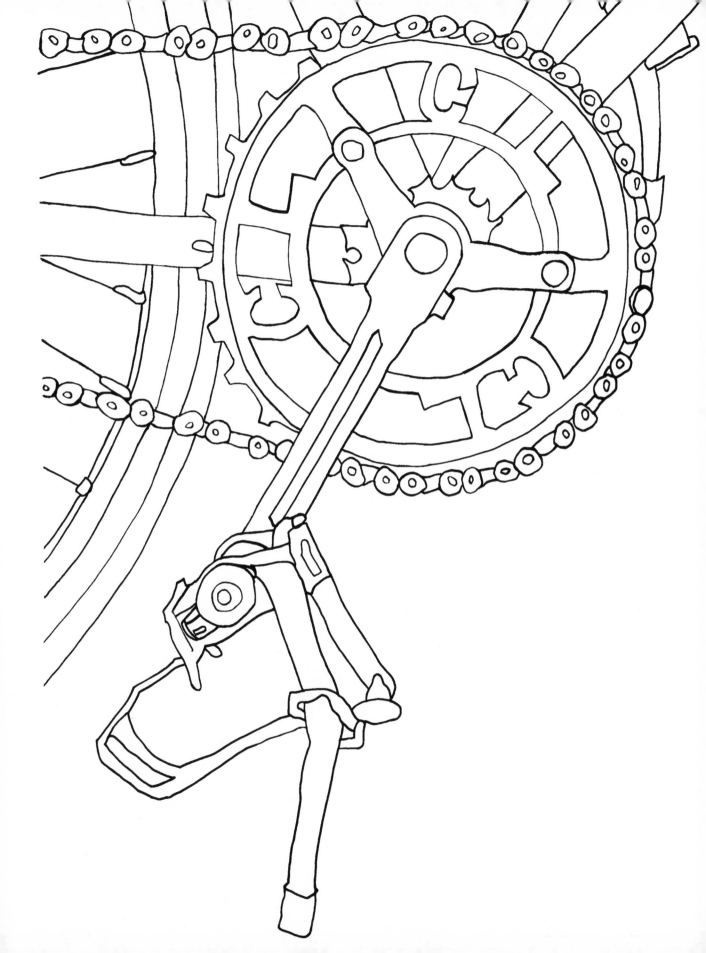

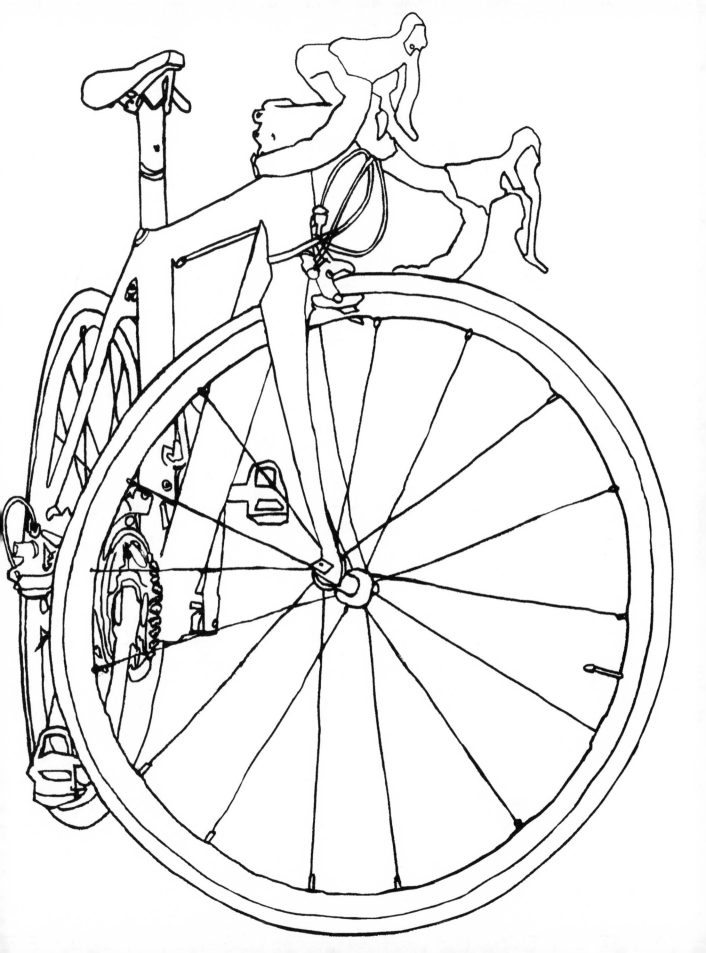

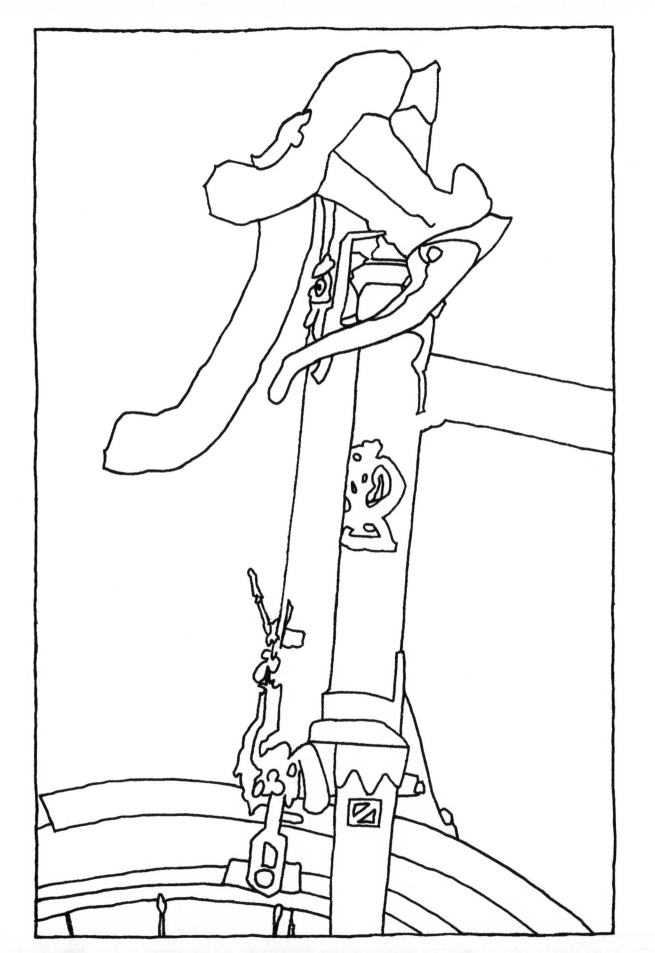

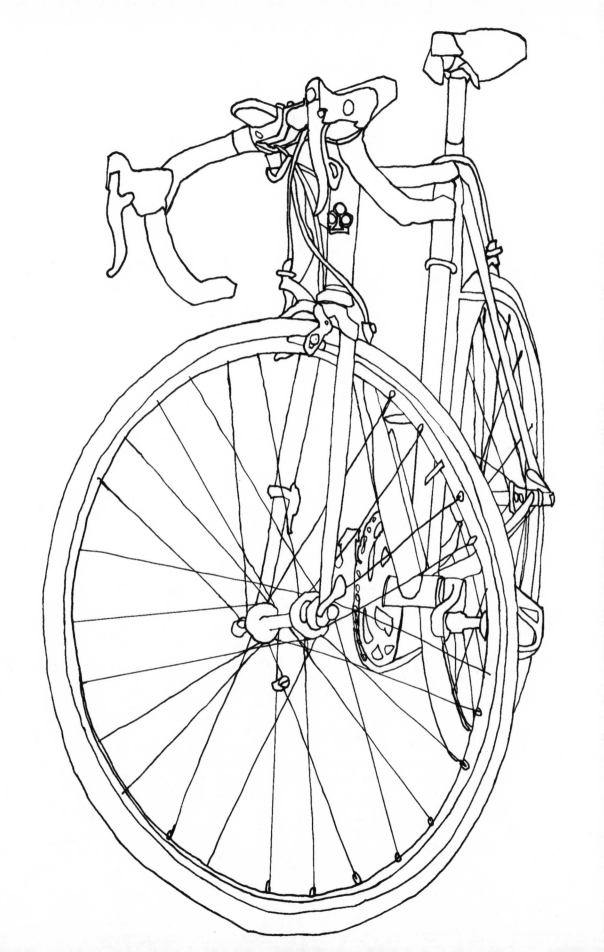

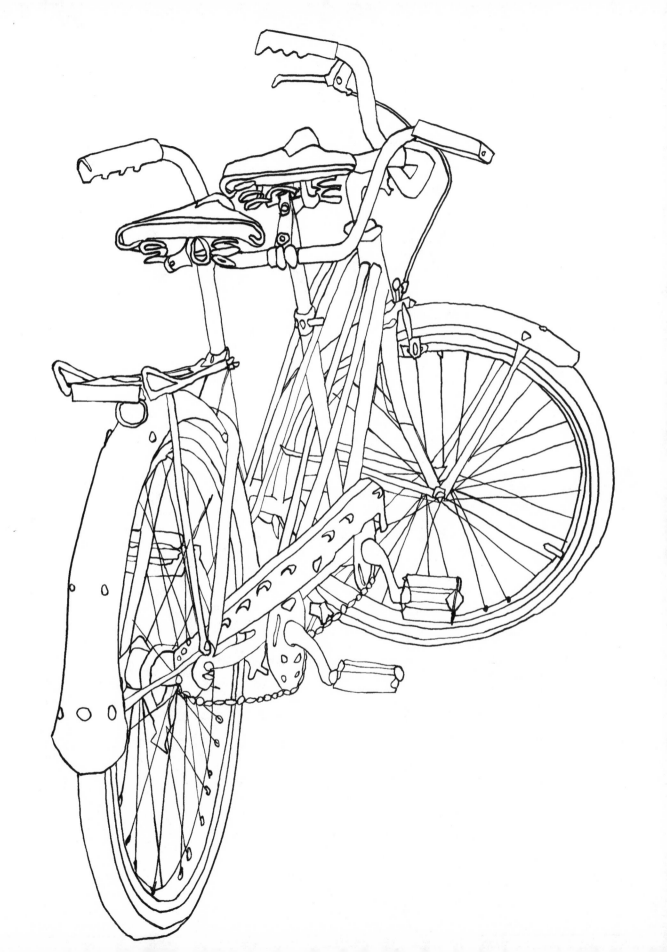

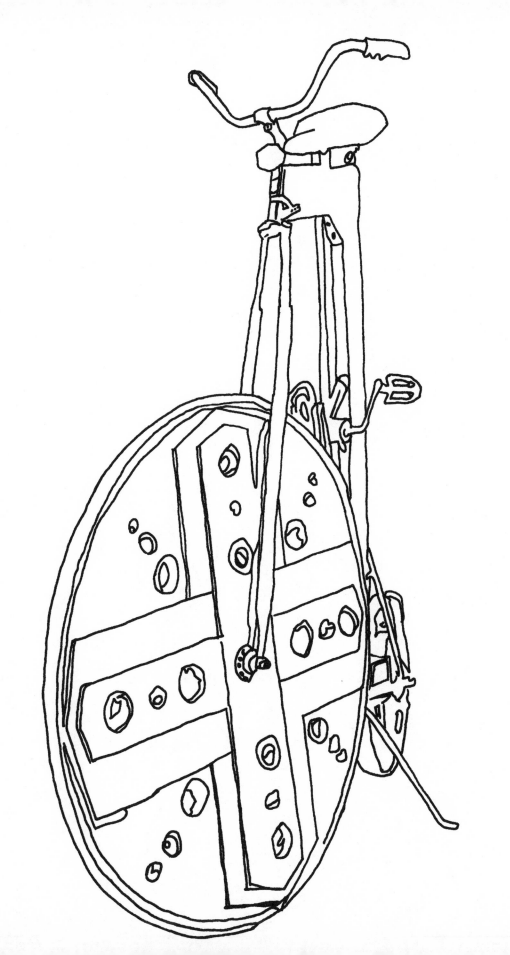

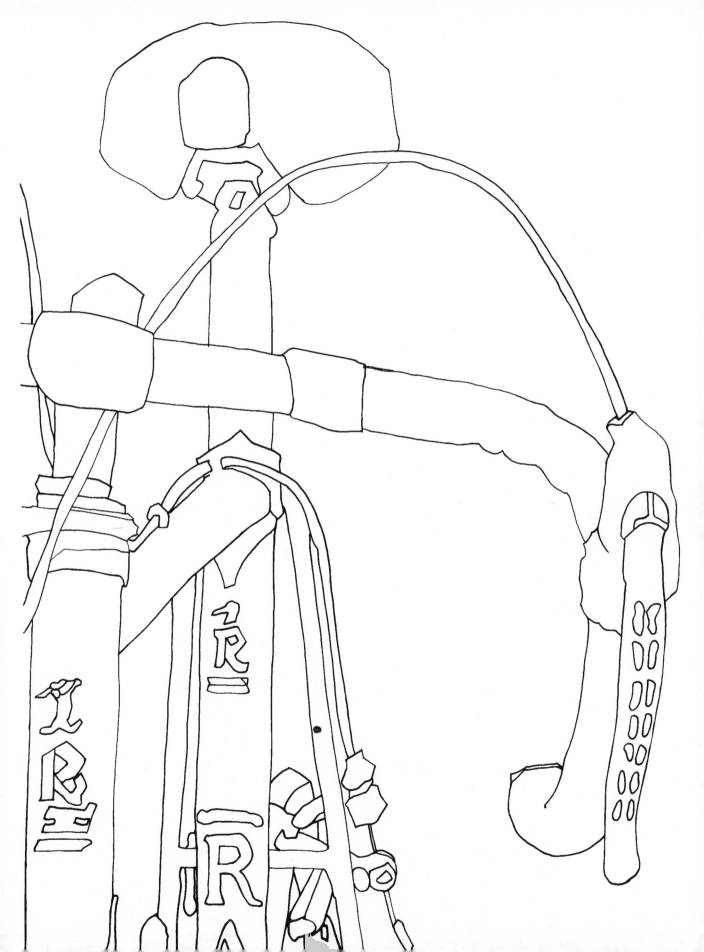

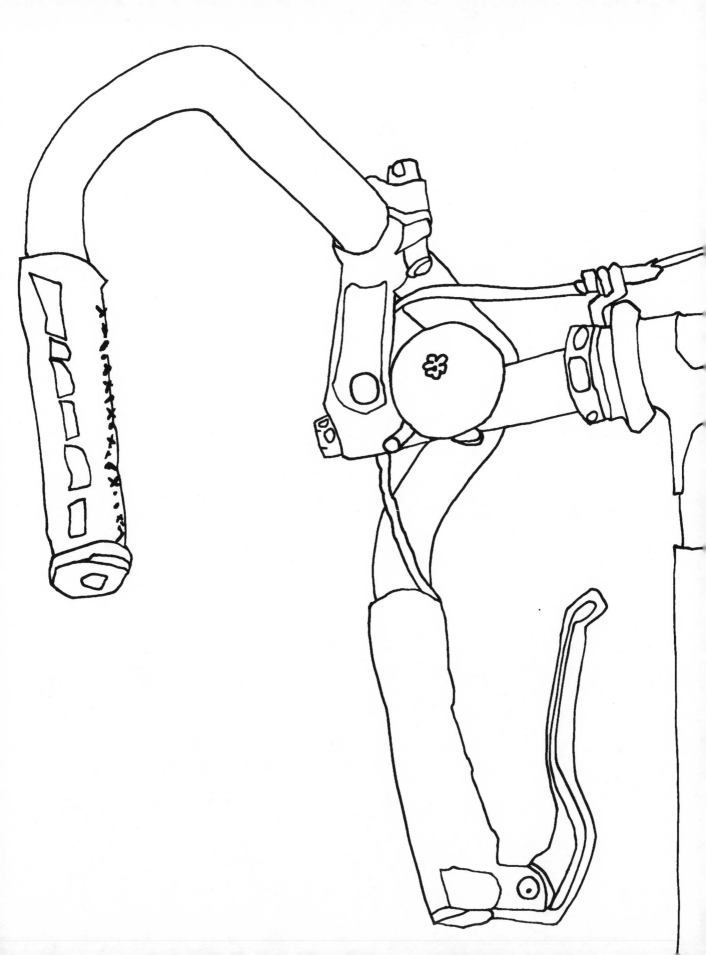

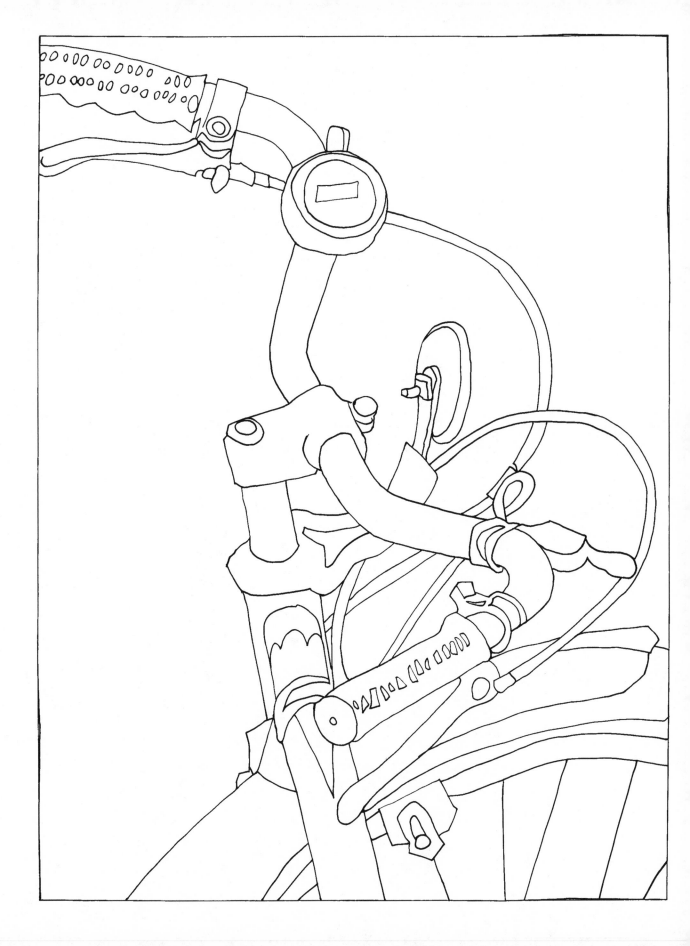

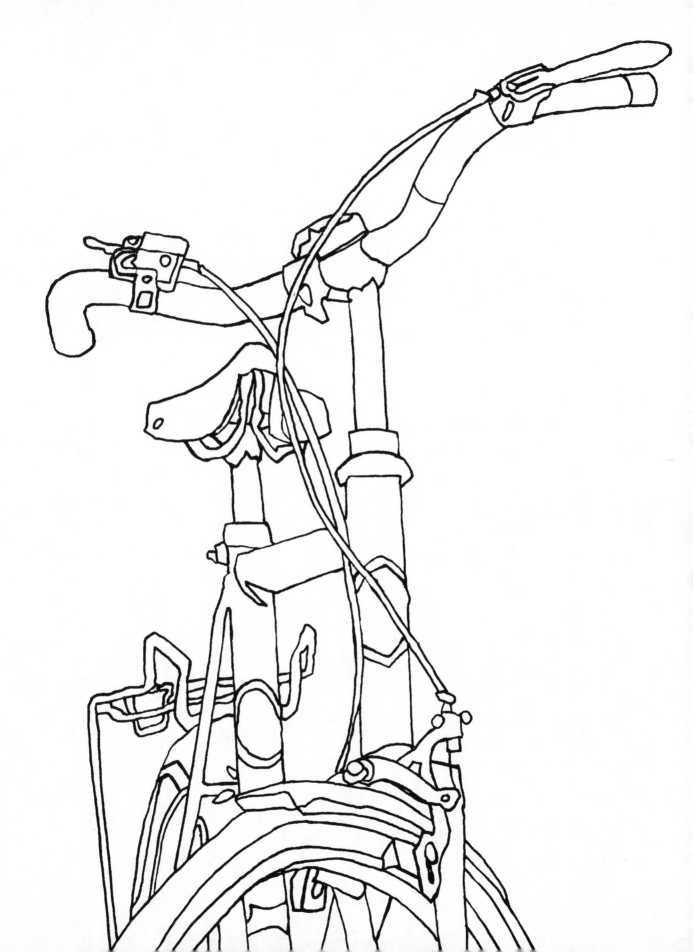

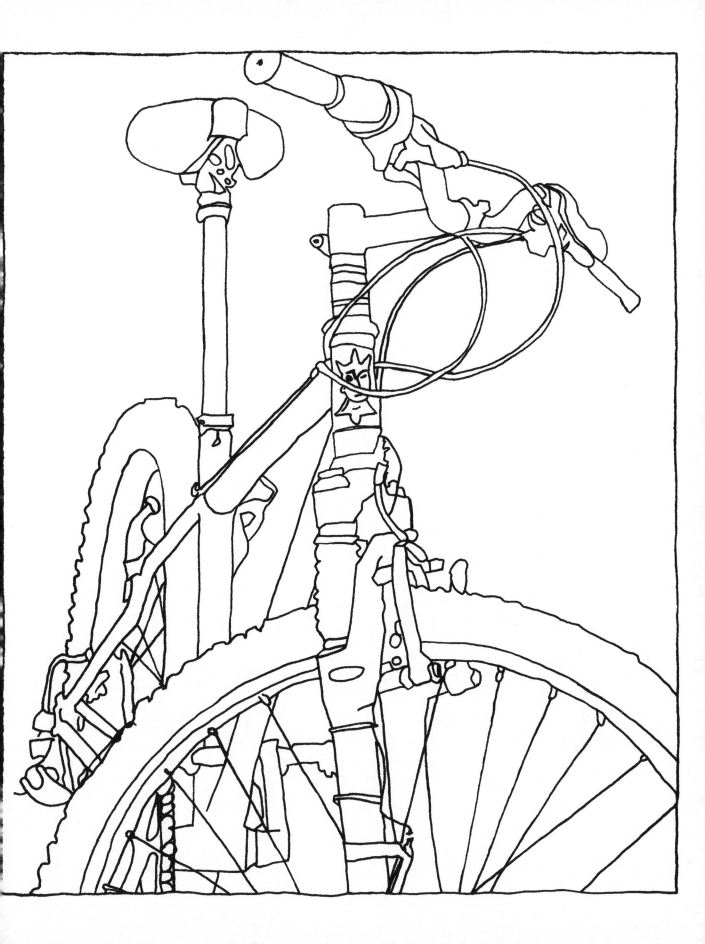

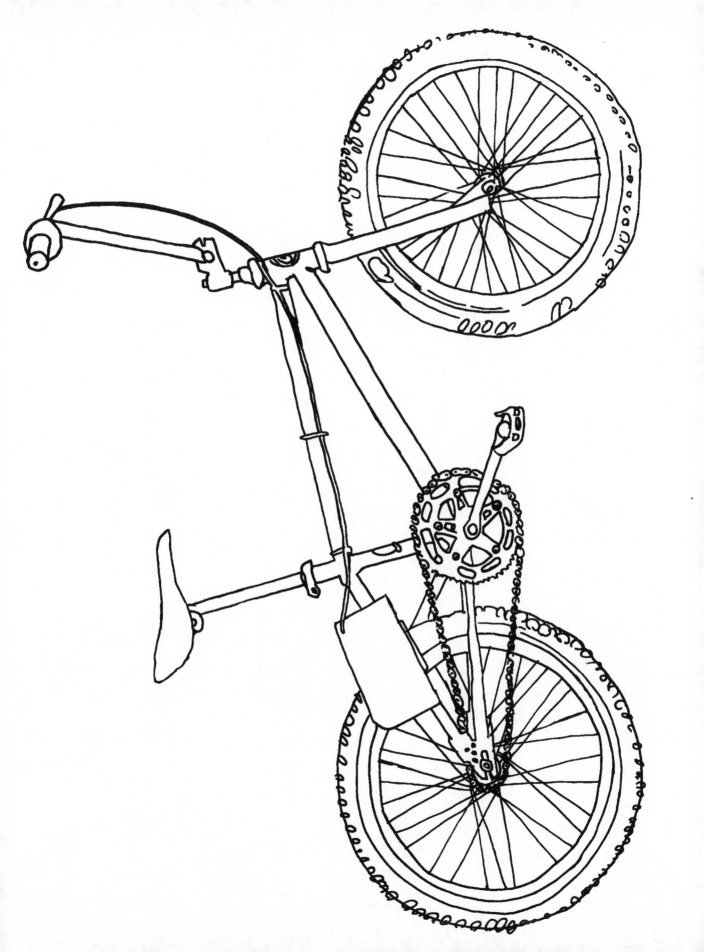

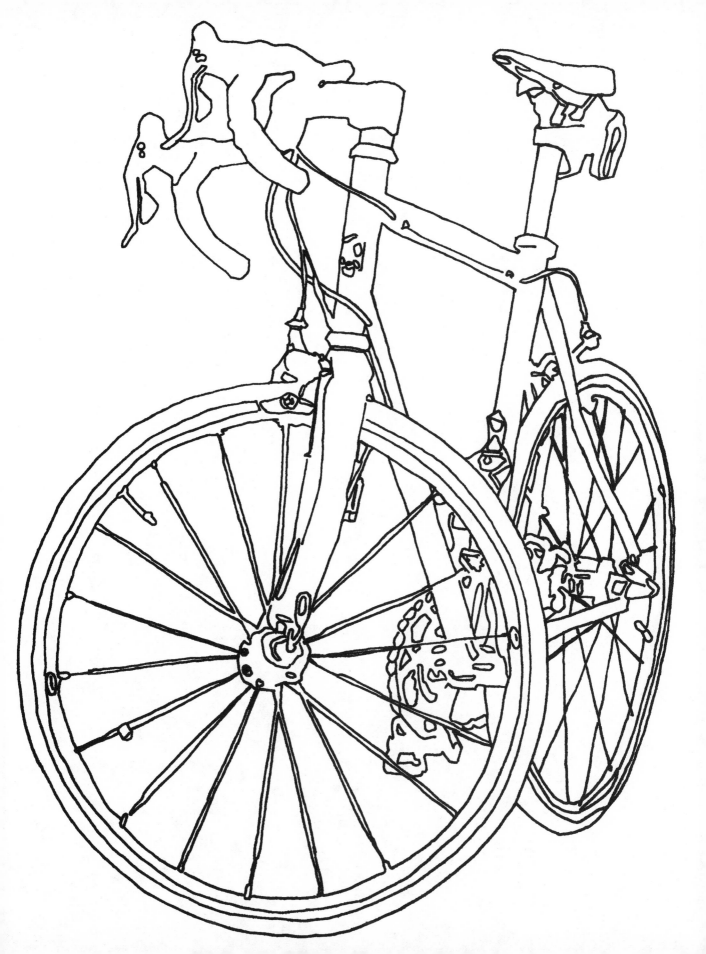

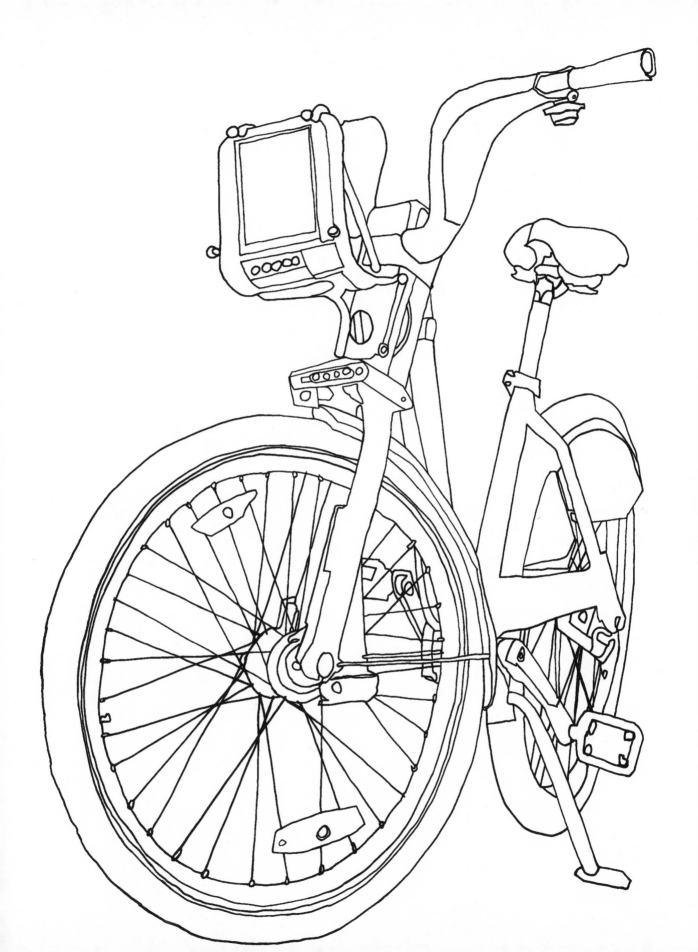

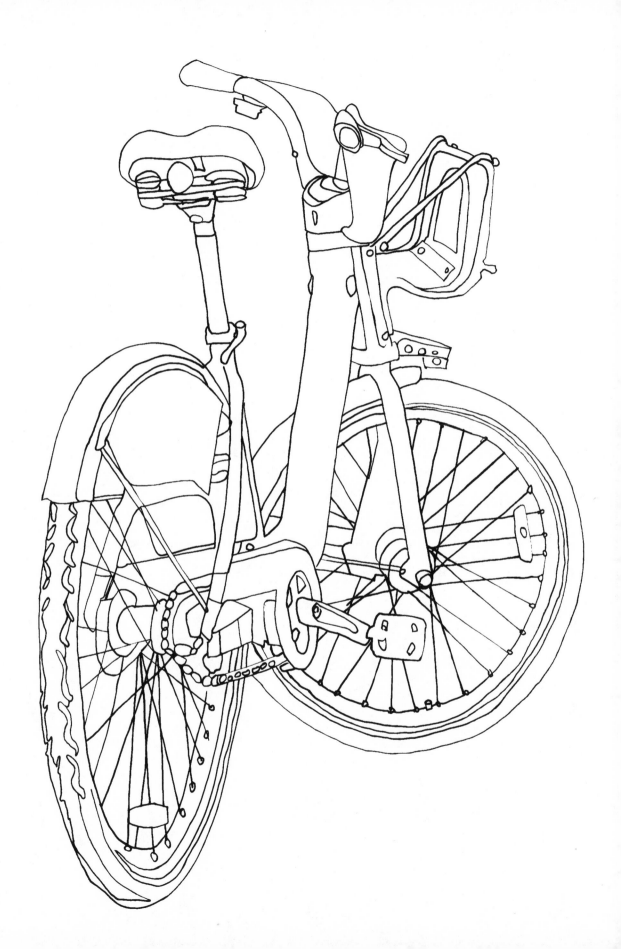

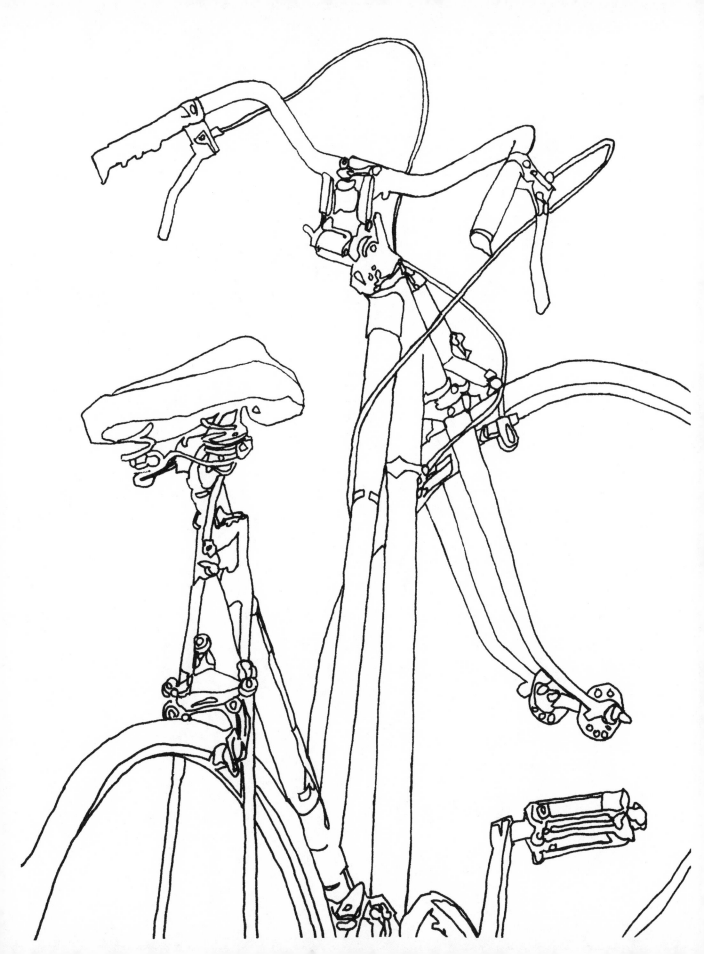

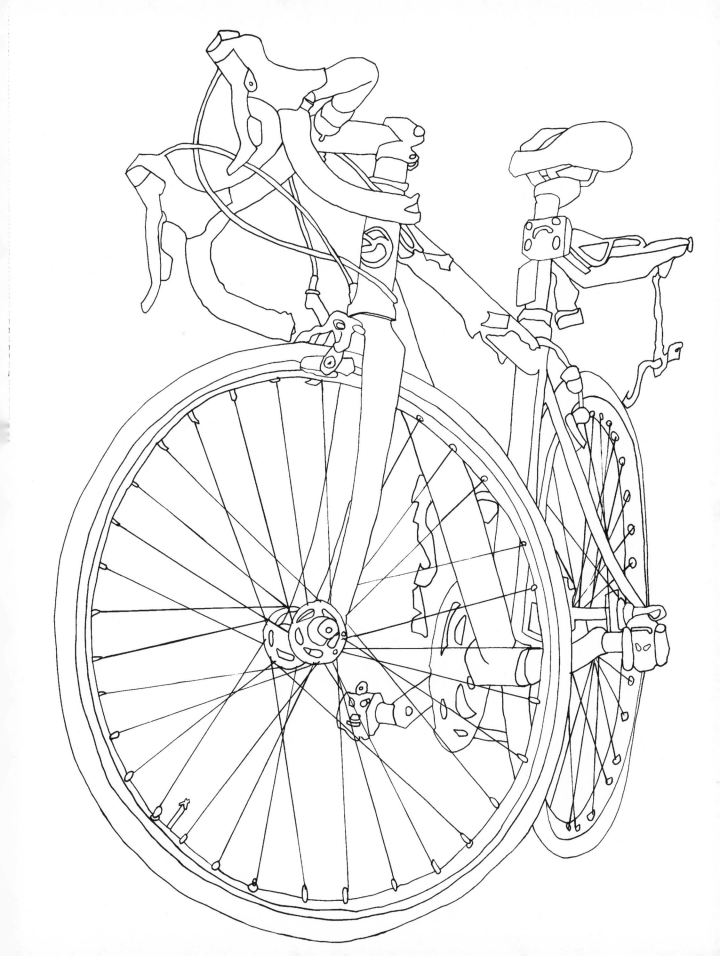

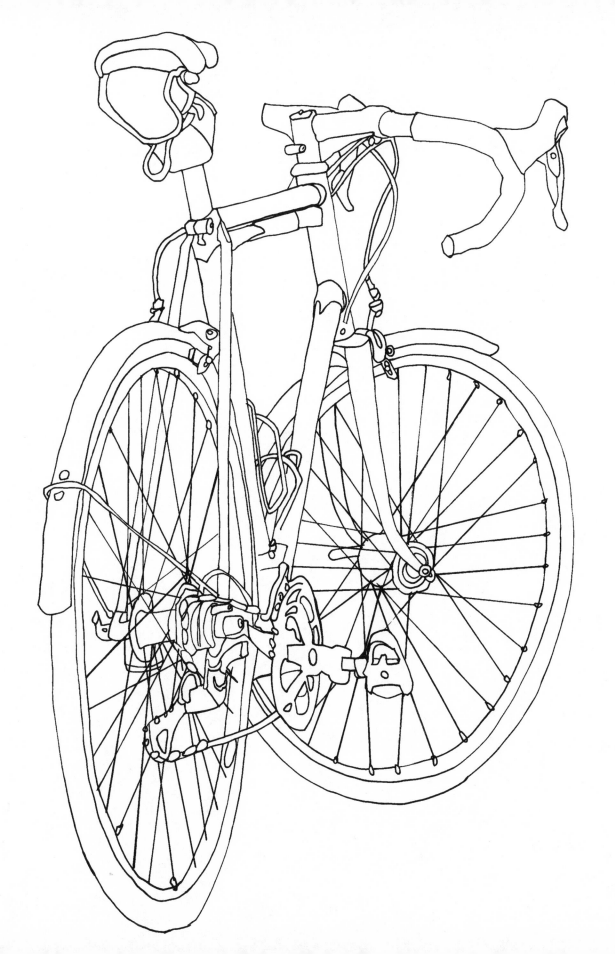

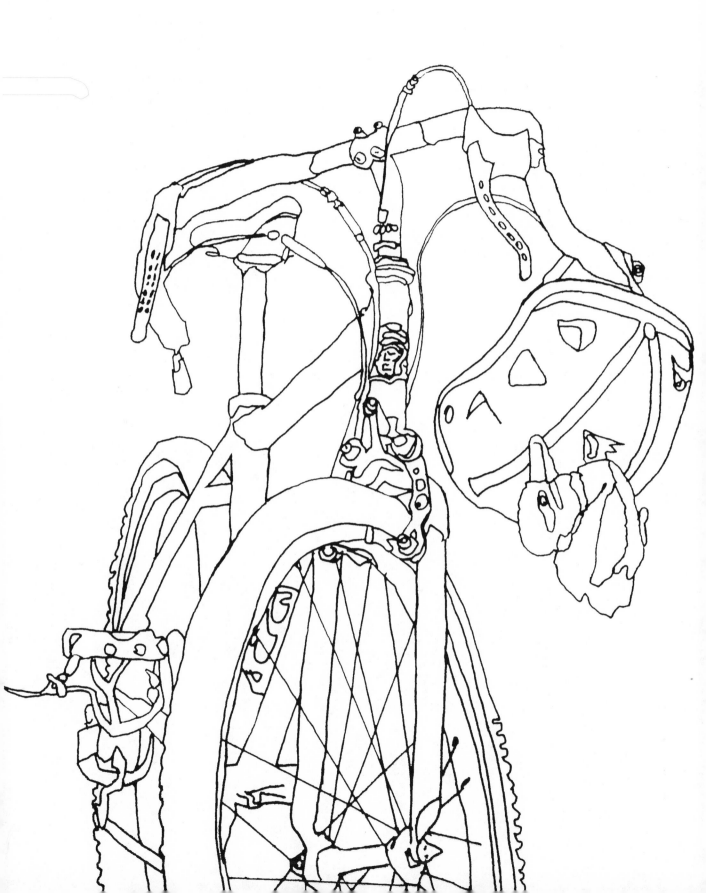

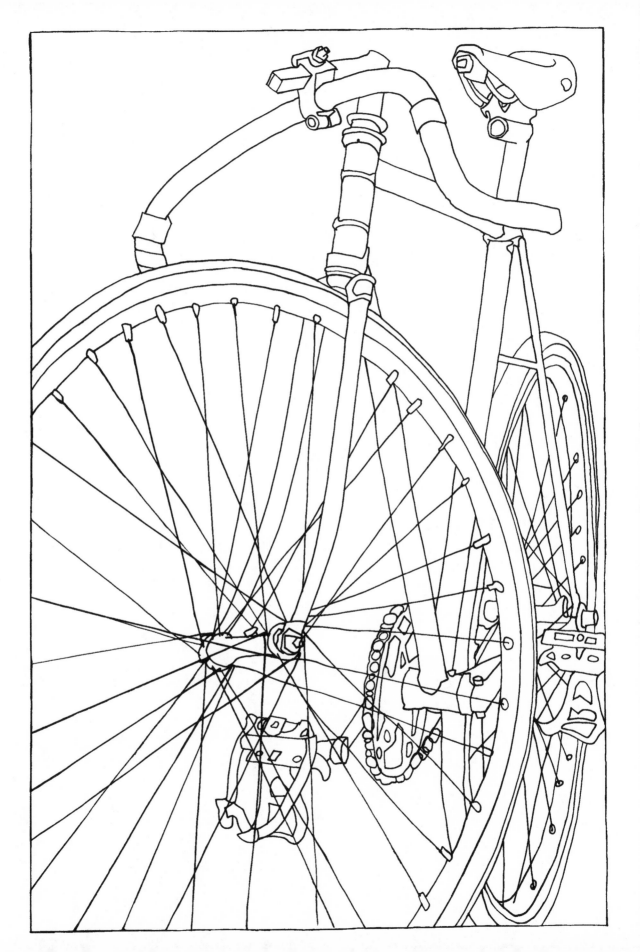

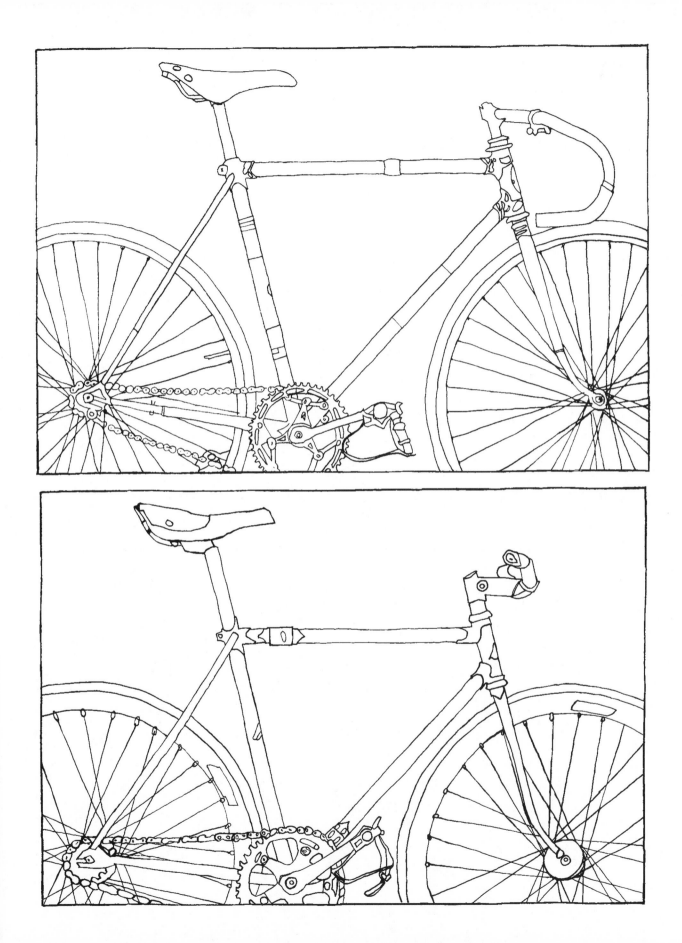

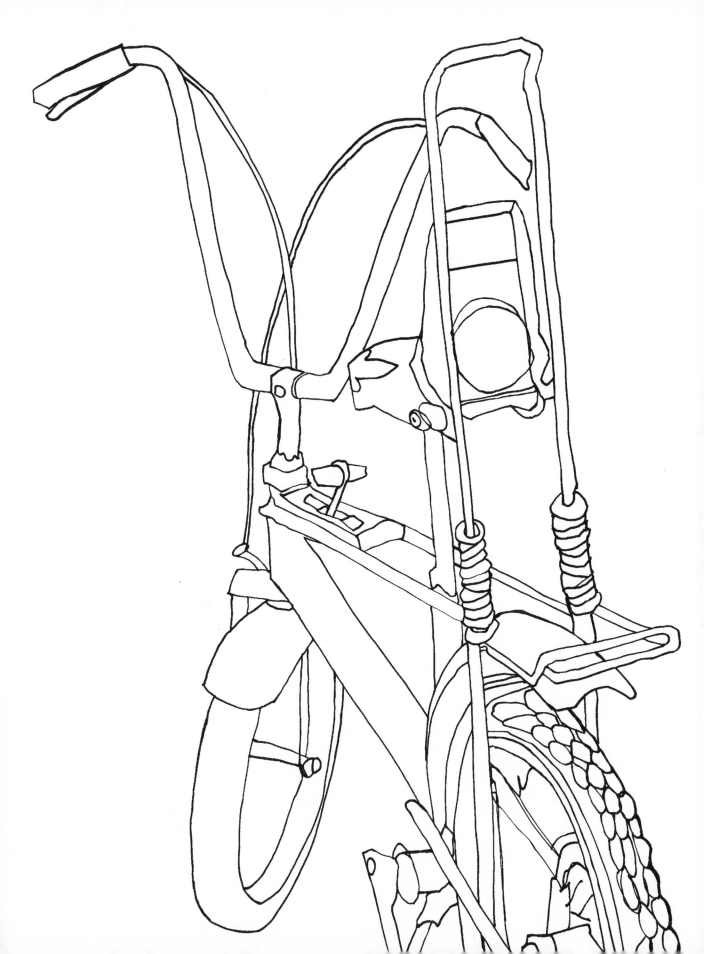

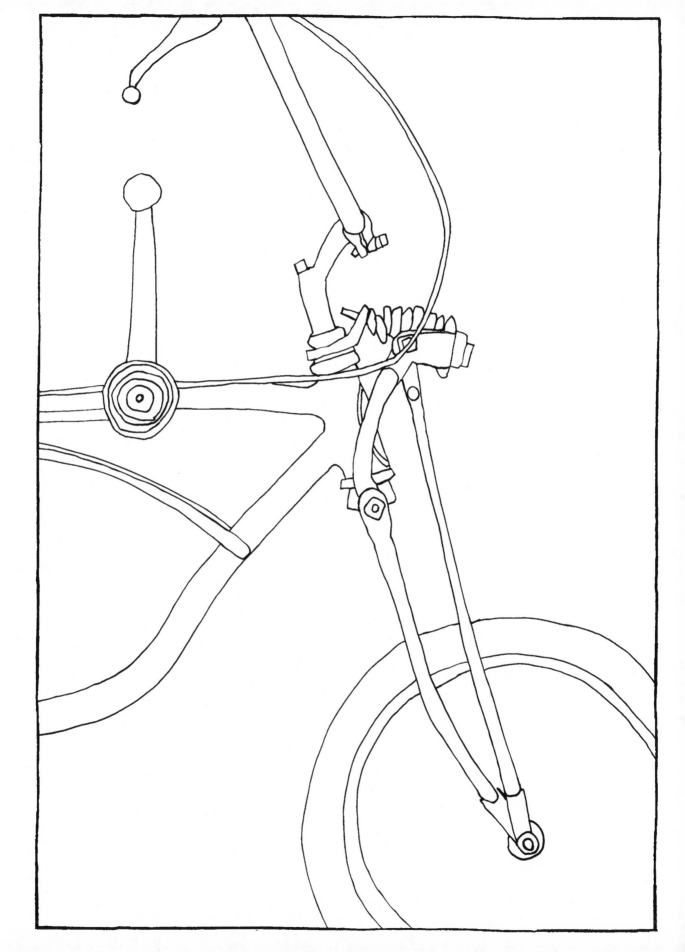

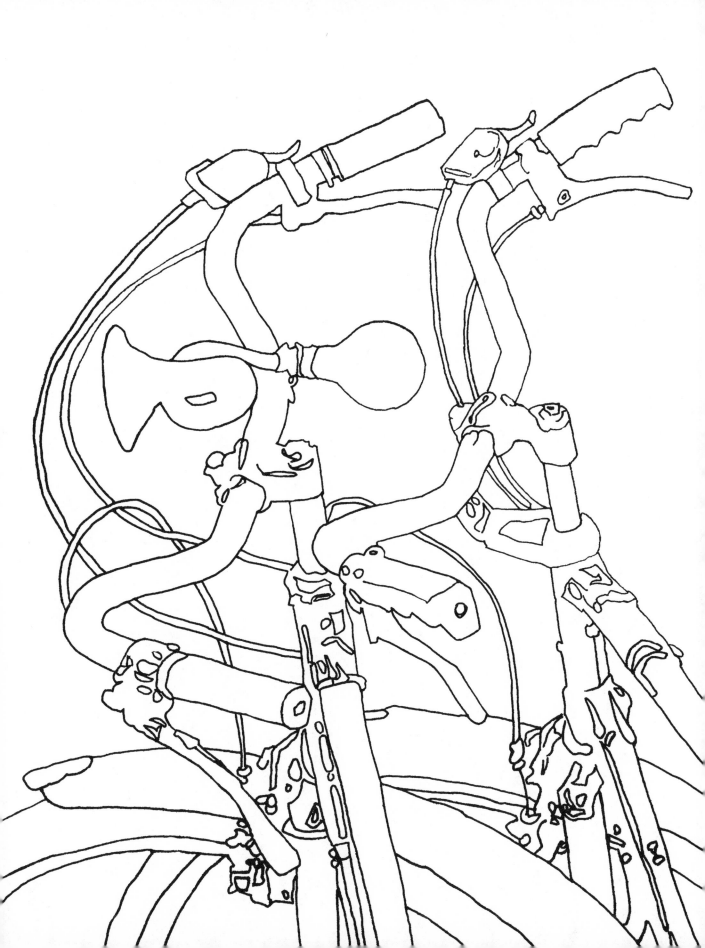

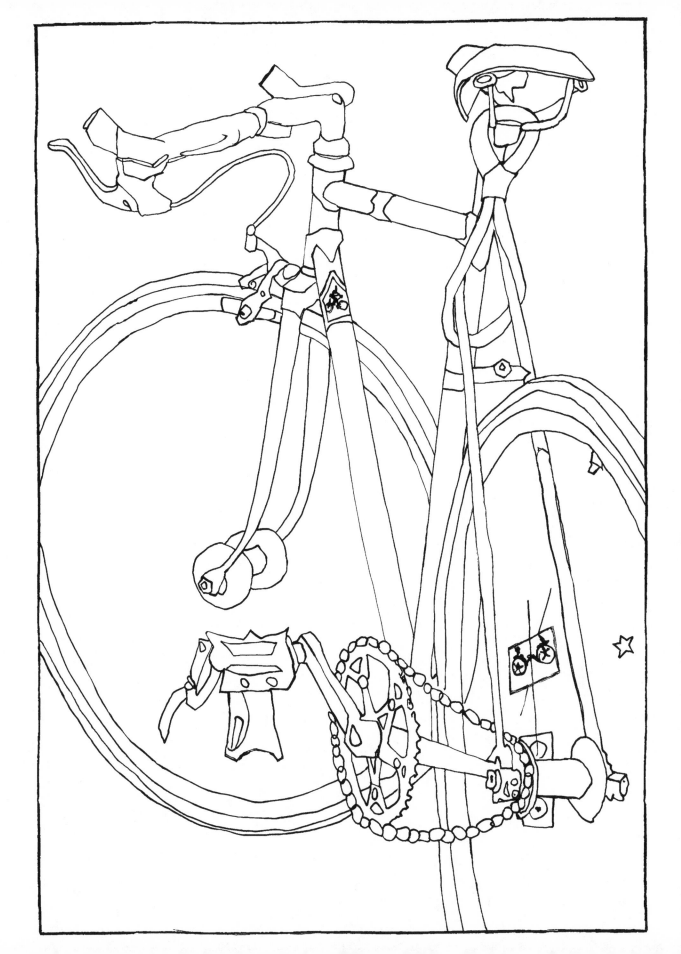

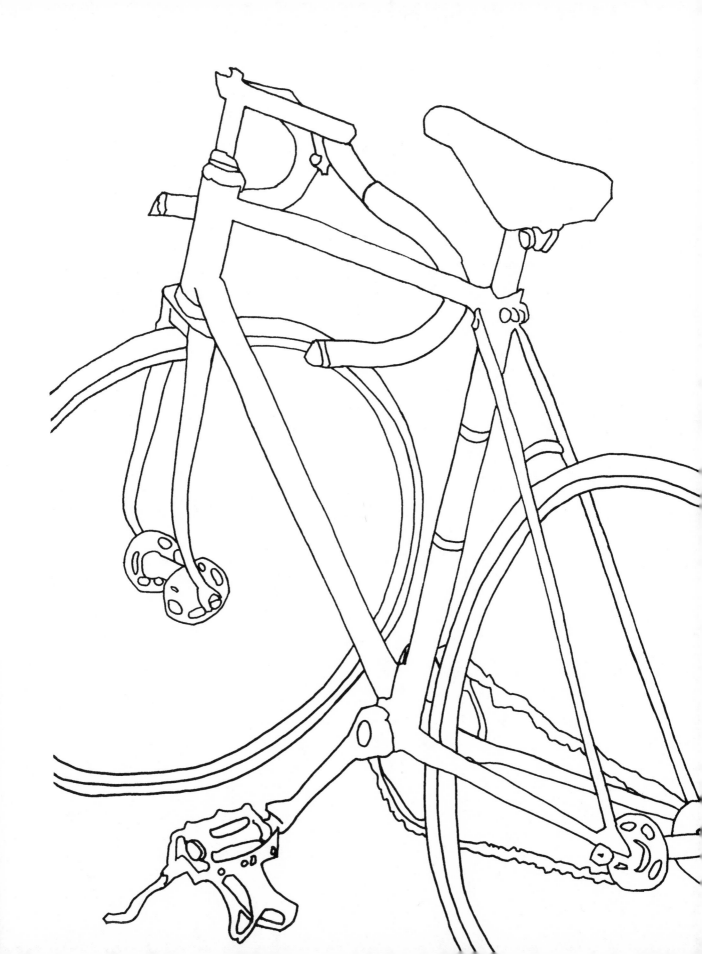

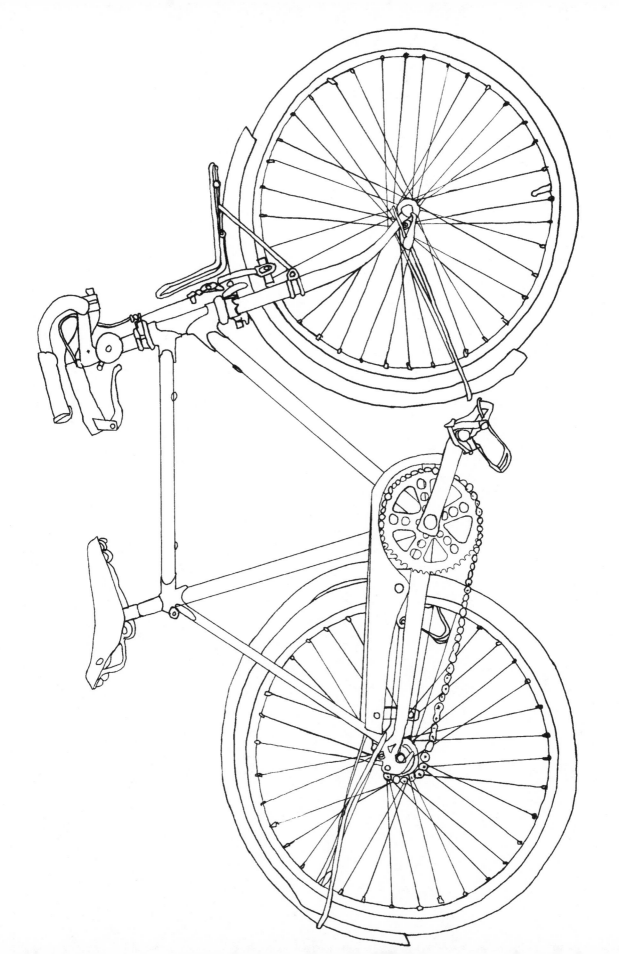

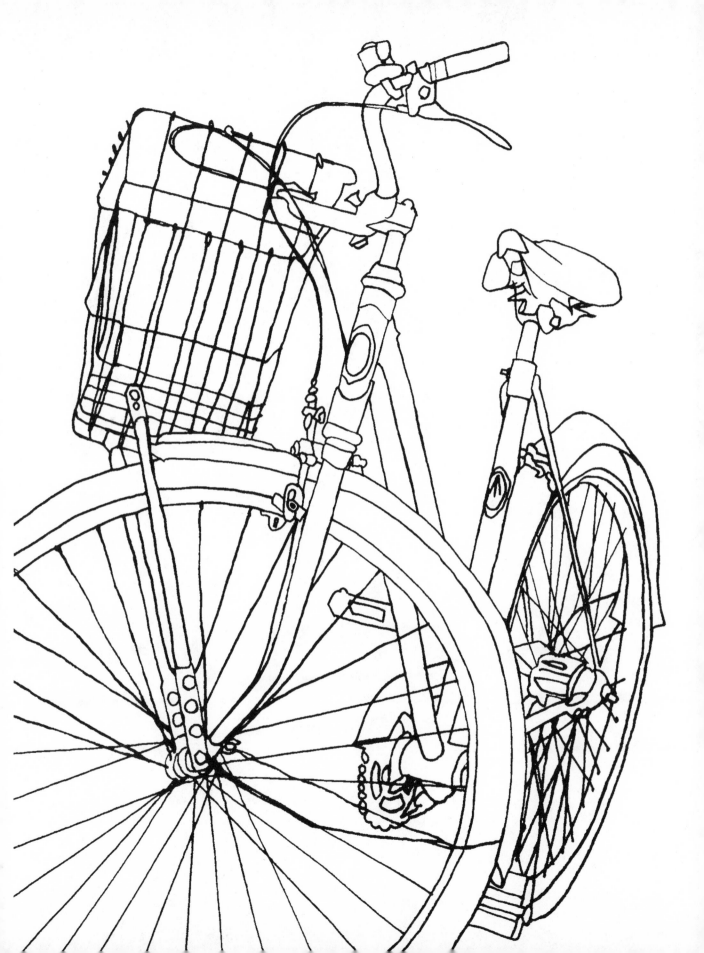

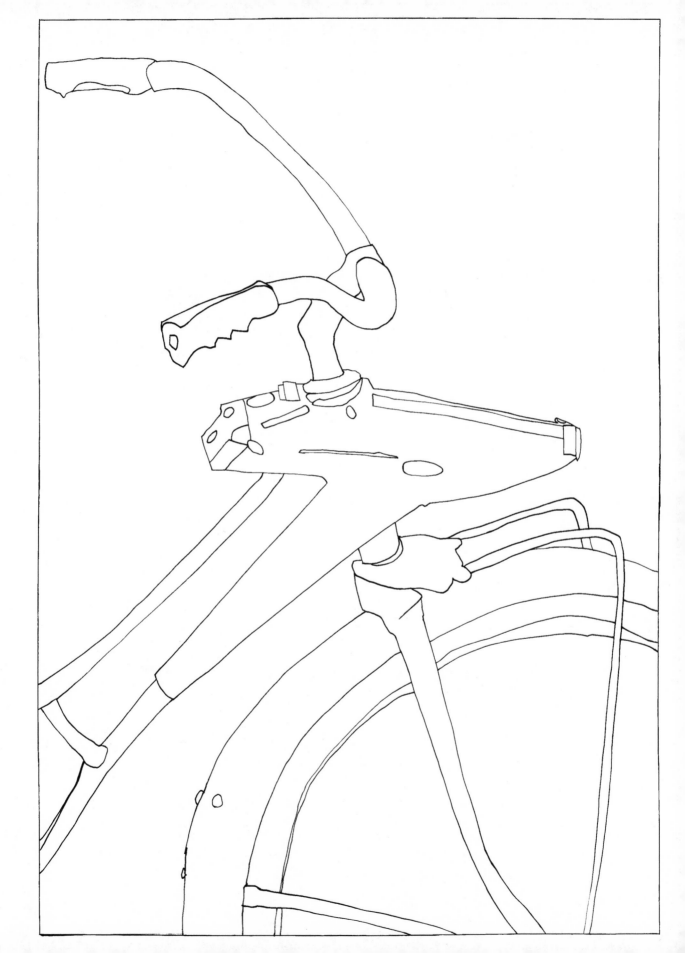

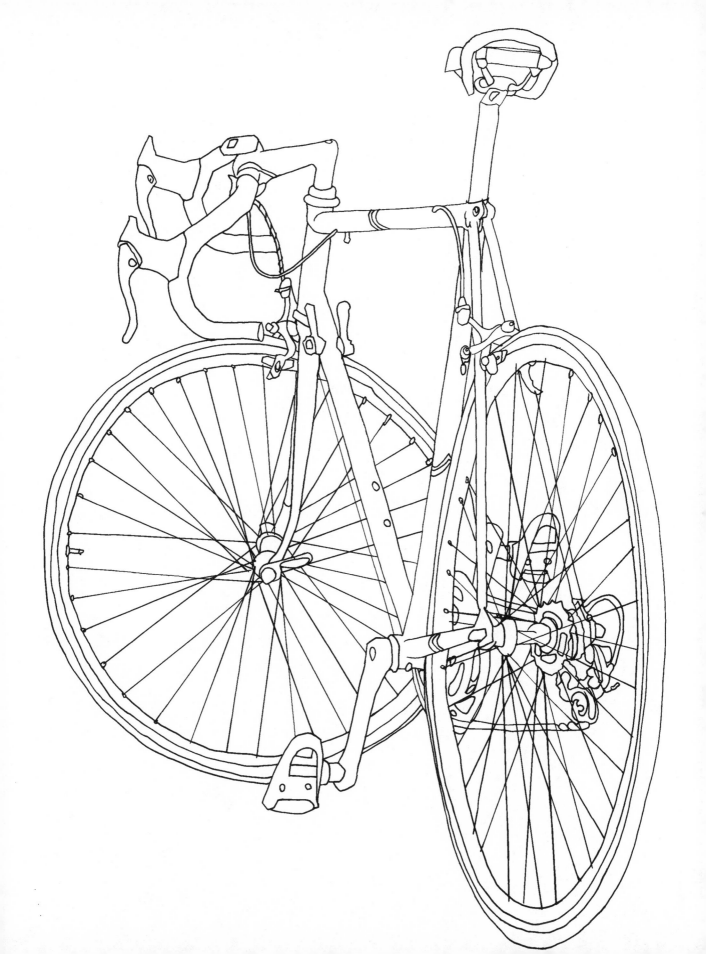

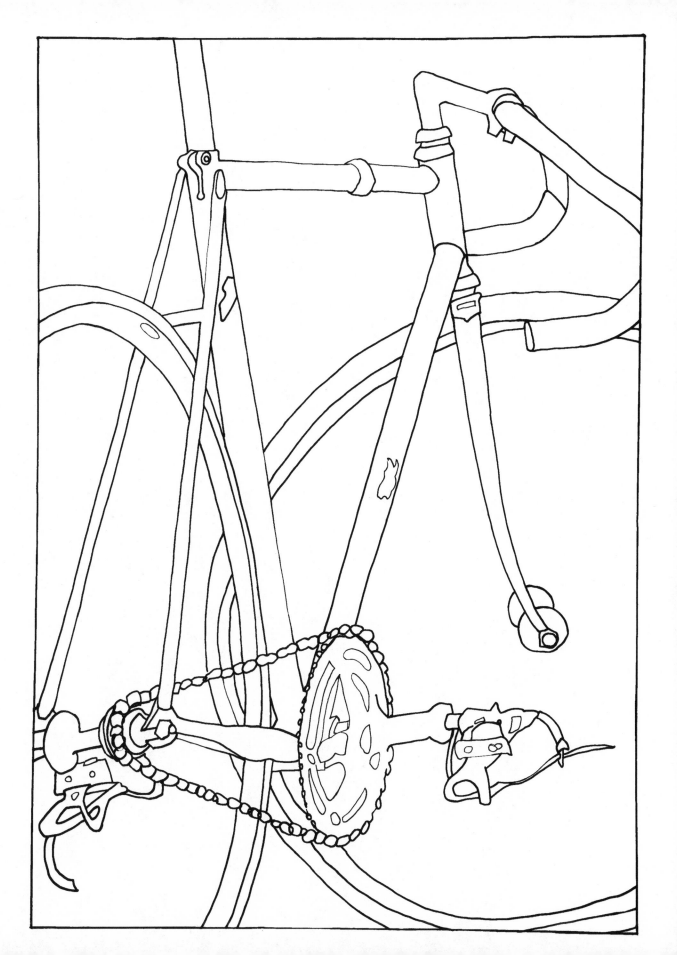

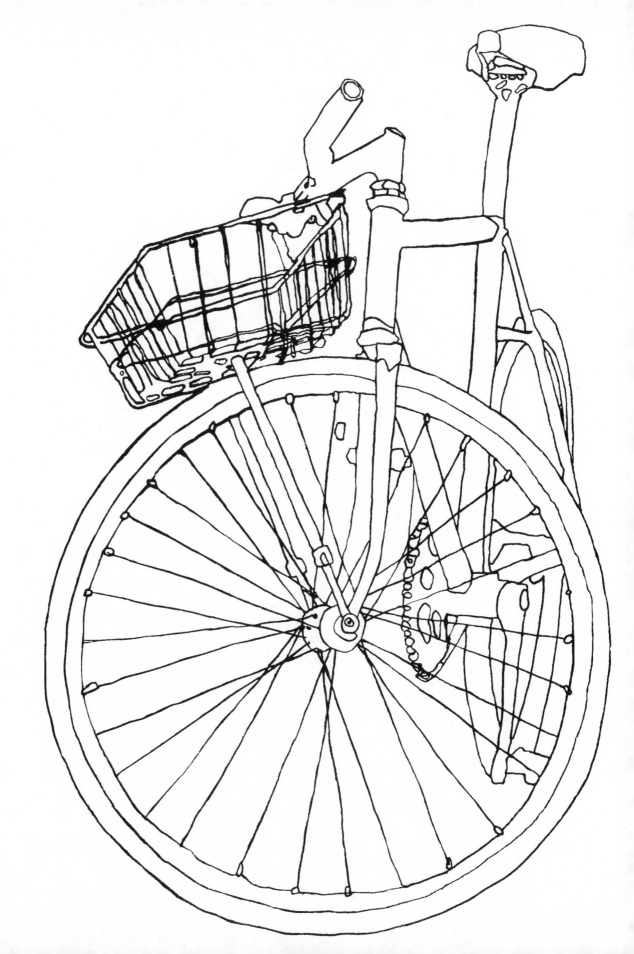

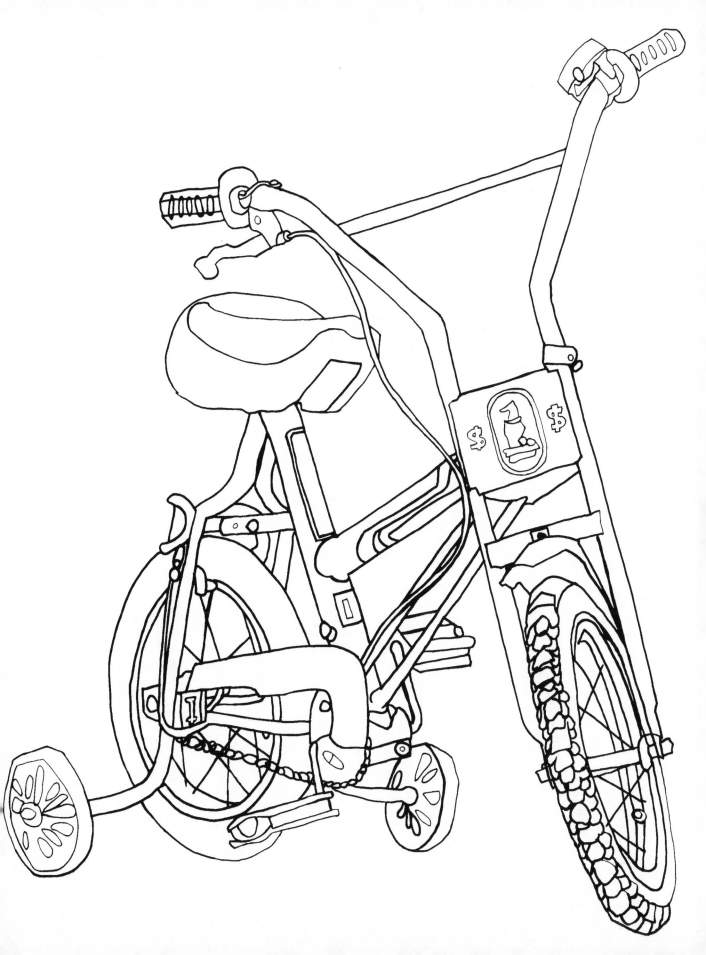

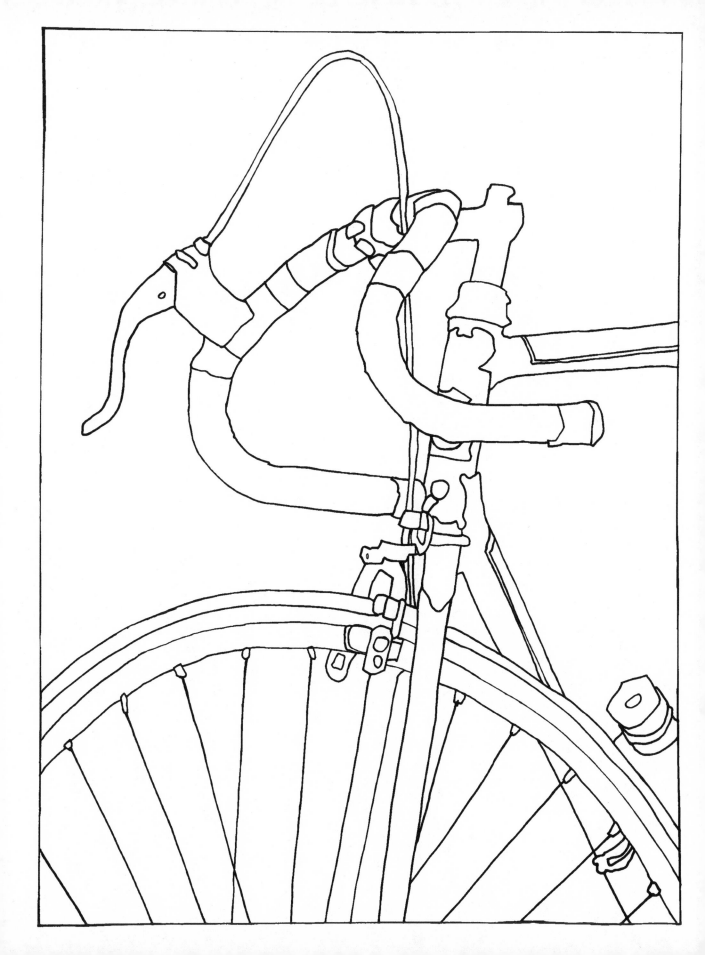

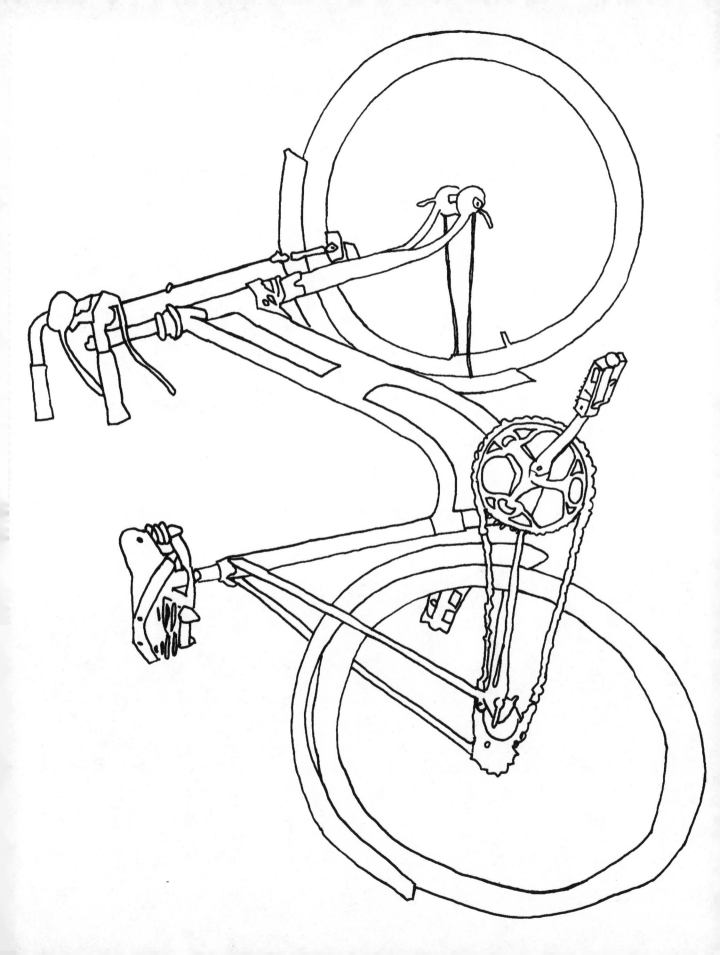

SUBSCRIBE TO EVERYTHING WE PUBLISH!

Do you love what Microcosm publishes?

Do you want us to publish more great stuff?

Would you like to receive each new title as it's published?

Subscribe as a BFF to our new titles and we'll mail them all to you as they are released!

$10-30/mo, pay what you can afford. Include your t-shirt size and your birthday for a possible surprise!

microcosmpublishing.com/bff

...AND HELP US GROW YOUR SMALL WORLD!

More gifts for the discerning radical person in your life:

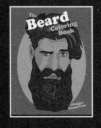
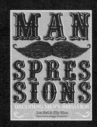
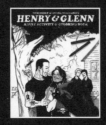
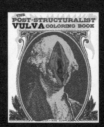
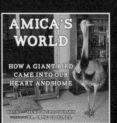
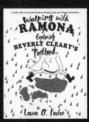